CW00972939

JANCIS
ROBINSON
ON
WINE

FINANCIAL TIMES

First published 1995
ISBN 1 85334 086 3

FINANCIAL TIMES

© The Financial Times

First published in the United Kingdom by
The Financial Times Limited
Number One Southwark Bridge
London SE1 9HL

Edited by
Eden Productions Limited
24 Belsize Lane
London NW3 5AB

Designed and produced by
Graffiti Editions Limited
7 Mitre House, 124 Kings Road
London SW3 4TR

Illustrations by Kim Dalziel

Typeset in Goudy. Printed and bound in Great Britain by
PJ Reproductions Ltd, Roslin Road, London W3 8DH

JANCIS
ROBINSON
ON
WINE

A SELECTION FROM
THE FINANCIAL TIMES
1990-95

Contents

SOBER THOUGHTS ON DRINKING ETIQUETTE

To what extent are we responsible for the actions of our guests when they are under the influence of what we have poured into their glasses? I have been fretting over this for some time now. However, I have been finally spurred into print on the subject by a reference to "host responsibility" in the monthly round robin sent to us wine writers by the most important man in wine-drinking Britain - Sainsbury's director of off-licence buying.

Allan Cheesman is one of the nation's more pragmatic wine enthusiasts. He throws this alarming concept at us and then - in the manner of old-fashioned sex educators - urges us to read the enclosed booklet. In this case it is "A Sainsbury's Guide to Low and No Alcohol", available at your local branch of our largest drink retailer.

Sainsbury's Alcohol Free Wine and Lambrusco Light Bianco, two of the nearly two dozen low- and no-alcohol beers and wines that the retailer can muster, may be facts of life but that doesn't make them any more palatable.

It will take more than the concept of host responsibility to persuade this host to substitute Palm Beach Mure ("subtly flavoured with blackberries") for the champagne I fear my guests have come to expect. Nonetheless, I do feel very responsible for the fact that when friends fall out of this front door, thanks to careful planning (and no little expense), they would make worse drivers than when they arrived.

Apart from the lager lout minority, people under 25 seem to me to have a much healthier attitude to drinking and driving than their parents. Genuinely scared of fines and endorsements, they were presumably caught at the right age by sensible alcohol education programmes and realise the folly taking to the steering wheel in their cups.

Older generations usually have the reassurance of several decades of drunken, or at least inebriated, driving behind them. They may well feel proud of their own driving skills, a pride that is only accentuated by a few comforting glasses. I know that before I looked into experiments contrasting driver confidence before and after alcohol intake, I used to believe I was a much better driver for two or three bracing units of alcohol. I am now convinced this is all a chimera and it's just not fair to inflict my delusions on other road users.

So without restricting our friends to those who have chauffeurs or investing heavily in sleeping bags, how are we to be socially responsible hosts?

I have felt particularly vulnerable on this score since writing a book constituting a consumers' guide to alcohol. The last thing I wanted - after so uncharitably pointing out that the alcohol in wine was the same as the alcohol in lager and vodka - was to seem a killjoy. I suspect that I have accordingly been killing my friends' livers with kindness, serving too much wine rather than too little in a dubious attempt to show that I haven't been completely swallowed up by prissiness.

We wine fanatics have an unhealthy habit of serving more than one wine at a time. It may enhance our understanding to compare two different vintages of the same wine, or two different examples of the same appellation, but it almost certainly leads us to consume more than we would if we drank wines one at a time like everybody else. I try to minimise such unthinking drinking by providing a jug for unwanted leftovers (before we move on to the next brace of bottles usually), but pouring away such expensive liquid goes against the grain for most people who are not forced by their livelihood to do just that.

A further complication is that the host of a domestic entertainment probably feels least like exercising personal restraint. He or she rarely has to operate machinery more dangerous than a dishwasher afterwards and may well feel more like preaching celebration than caution. Although we try to plan minicabs for our return journeys, I draw the line at imposing this discipline on others. Perhaps it is a subconscious move to shame befuddled friends into good behaviour, but I am not aware of it.

I cannot imagine sanctimoniously relieving friends of their car keys saying: "Now now, let's just settle down to an hour or five of Trivial Pursuit and coffee until we've got that blood alcohol level down a bit, shall we?"

Those who live in towns with flourishing taxi and minicab services, and good public transport systems are lucky - we have genuine alternatives to that last resort, abstinence. I can quite see that host responsibility takes on quite a different complexion in the depths of the country. I suppose guest lists could be compiled with geography in mind so that four guests, say, would need only one sober driver - but think how they'd gossip on the way back. Bring on the sleeping bags.

Long before you appoint yourself moral guardian of your guests, there are some simple provisions the thoughtful, responsible host should make.

Be particularly wary of the effects of alcohol on an empty stomach. The aperitif will almost certainly be the most potentially dangerous drink you serve, particularly if it's champagne (which hits the system with greatest force, thanks to the gas) and if you serve no food to soften the blow. The Weekend FT's revered wine correspondent Edmund Penning-Rowsell introduced us to the golden rule of serving something to nibble with champagne. Roka cheese biscuits (sold by Waitrose) go beautifully and are good and fatty.

Always offer a non-alcoholic alternative, Sainsbury's Light Lambrusco Bianco if you must. I have yet to drink a no- or low-alcohol wine with pleasure - although I can happily stomach their beer equivalents (perhaps because I have a less keen appreciation of how they ought to taste). Be aware of the gulf that effectively yawns between no-alcohol and low-alcohol products. Many low-alcohol wines are deliciously sweet and grapey but can be more than half as alcoholic as normal wine - so should not be swigged the way alcohol-free wines can be. The alcohol content should be marked on the label. Less than one per cent means swiggable.

Even for those who are drinking, please put a water glass on the table as a matter of course - and keep on filling it. I try to drink as much water as wine. If I ever find myself slaking a thirst with wine then I know I'm heading for trouble.

In a final plea for "guest responsibility", I would urge that everyone decides how they will get home, even if it simply means deciding who will be the driver, before the first glasses are filled. It takes about an hour for one "unit" of alcohol (a smallish glass of wine) to work through the system. If a typical man drinks six units over three hours and a typical woman four, their blood alcohol level will probably be under the legal limit for drivers, but abstinence is the wisest course. Remember the unwelcome fact that a really heavy evening's drinking can leave a driver's system too thoroughly awash with alcohol to be safe the morning after.

January 15, 1990

Farr- The Sweet Bouquet of Success

Margaret Thatcher might consider using Stephen Browett in any future advertising campaign to persuade young people to learn a foreign language. At 30, he and his 32 year-old partner Lindsay Hamilton have developed Farr Vintners into a company selling some £7m a year of the finest and rarest wines, not much less than Christie's. The leap into the big time by this unconventional pair owes much to Browett's year as a student in Nimes. This left him better equipped to grapple with the complexities of buying - mainly at auction in Paris, Belgium and Geneva - than counterparts who were less capable linguistically (and, possibly, less ambitious). As he says: "There are people in the UK selling very important wines who don't speak French. You couldn't possibly go to an auction in France unless you spoke French. I picked up some very useful things because the French aren't as vintage-conscious as we are."

Browett joined Farr in September 1984. He had worked previously as a van driver for a somewhat pin-striped Chelsea wine merchant but, during his first six months with the new company, spent every weekend snooping around northern Europe, buying goodies unimagined by Farr's rivals and making valuable contacts with customers and suppliers. The Farr style is the opposite of pin-striped: Hamilton is distinctly cocky, although he says: "I was supposed to be the black sheep but I've really mellowed." He is the one who is good with Farr's pop star customers.

But it was Browett whom one wine auctioneer remembers patrolling the aisles at a sale in Geneva giving out business cards. Browett's injection of fine wine from the continent could not have come at a better time for Farr Vintners. The dollar and sterling were strong against the French franc, the 1982 red bordeaux vintage was being hyped to the skies in the US and, as Browett puts it: "Even if you didn't buy very well, you could sell very well then." Thanks to this boom, Hamilton's sales patter and Browett's buying diligence, Farr's turnover quadrupled to £3m in 1985 (although other fine wine traders and brokers also did well).

The more conventional in the wine trade have long been wary of brokers. It was assumed that, like circles of fine art traders in many other fields, the same goods were listed by several different brokers who traded between themselves at cost to the eventual buyer.

However, Browett and Hamilton claim they are traders, not brokers. They showed me their latest list, marked "Confidential" - including a right-hand column which customers never see showing who owns what they offer for sale.

Unless they had carefully doctored and then distressed this well-thumbed document in honour of my visit, it would appear that they own a good 90 per cent of their £850,000 worth of fine wine stock. Indeed, the wine departments at Sotheby's and Christie's both have named Farr Vintners as their most important customer (although the head of Christie's wine department spoke to these be-sneakered youths for the first time only three years ago).

Now that the boys have made good, they have just moved to premises in Pimlico more in keeping with their station than the couple of converted bedrooms in Hamilton's house. This might have forced them into an overdraft for the first time in five years, but the proper shop-front should now seem presentable to visiting foreign collectors - although, presumably, the proprietors would be horrified by anyone wandering in looking for a bottle of Liebfraumilch. Browett and his wife will live above the office so he is the one who will get to check the fax machine for orders during dinner two or three times a night.

The company was formed in 1978 by Jim Farr, who had worked for a brewery-owned wine shipper for five years and decided to punt £5,000 borrowed from his mother on a small venture of his own. It specialised in burgundy, because everyone else seemed to be long on bordeaux. Hamilton was recruited as a 21-year-old from Harrods' wine department where he had spent two years, having asked for a transfer from china.

Farr was bought out last July, leaving Hamilton to specialise in burgundy and selling and Browett to consolidate his reputation as the scourge of the auction houses. He claims to have attended every important London sale for the past six years (although he missed the last one I enquired about), and both auction houses agree that he can be their most demanding customer in terms of condition of bottles, fill levels (ullage) and general agreement with catalogue descriptions. In their old office, Farr had a fireplace filled with bottles waiting to be returned to Christie's or Sotheby's with some complaint. The company now keeps its stock at Trapps Cellars by London Bridge, as do Christie's and Sotheby's, to minimise movement of the fragile commodity. According to John Heather of Trapps, itself a treasure trove of fine wine belonging to hundreds of different collectors: "Stephen is a very bright lad indeed. He knows his wines, he knows his customers and he's a tremendous ferreter. We have to stop him ferreting about too much in here; his eyes are everywhere."

Farr's list is deep but narrow, with *grands formats* - giant bottles suitable for giant feasts - a speciality. You can't buy fewer than 12 bottles from the company's list and the bill could be £6,200 for six magnums of Château Pétrus 1953. Guigal Gigondas 1985, at £55 a case in bond, is about as low, and about as exotic, as they go.

The partners say they have tried properties and vintages they knew were delicious, under-rated and under-priced. But such wines are for the likes of us, rather than the company chairman worth £350 an hour cited by Browett as a typical customer who "just knows he wants Pétrus. Originally, we'd be more idealistic and buy wines we really liked; but then we realised that, to be successful, you have to have what people are looking for. And, in some cases, that can be one single property. We have some customers who'll buy, for instance, nothing but Cheval Blanc."

The bulk of their sales are, however, to fellow traders, most notably mature bordeaux sold back to merchants in Bordeaux. "The worst way to run a wine company is to go to Bordeaux to buy bordeaux," they maintain (pointing out with some pride that, since they tipped '86 clarets, eschewing '85s, the price of the former has streaked away). Many of their personal favourites come from the Rhône. Browett served the relatively rustic Châteauneuf-du-Pape, Château de Beaucastel 1981, at his wedding. They never drink during the working day now (too many international phone calls) and, although they reckon to have tasted just about all the "greats" between them, they say there is no point in opening a really good bottle of wine for fewer than six people.

"You can get jaded," says Hamilton. "We had a dinner not long ago when everyone brought one of the greatest wines of the world - Mouton '45, a Chevalier-Montrachet '71, that sort of thing. It shocked us afterwards that we couldn't remember every one. You really need to build up to great wine."

Great wines are becoming scarce, especially from classic vintages such as 1961 and 1945, but that might do Farr no harm. "A lot of people in the British wine trade may know more about wine than us, but they're not necessarily very good at being wine merchants," Hamilton adds.

Having seen Browett put in the hard physical work required by the organisation of a complex wine tasting, I think he must have been as assiduous a van driver as he is a wine trader. It must be strange to have people pleading for an allocation of a particularly rare bottling who, only six years before, were asking you to wipe your shoes before struggling over their threshhold under the weight of a case or two for the cellar.

"I still remember people I delivered to. Even if they come on the phone wanting 20 cases of DRC [Domaine de la Romanée-Conti] burgundy, I never forget what they were like to me then," says Browett, with a tight-lipped smile. You know what he means.

Farr Vintners, 19 Sussex Street, London SW1 (Tel: 0171 828 1960). Other fine wine traders include Whitwhams, Old Market Place, Altrincham (0161 928 9416); Turville Valley Wines, The Firs, Potter Row, Great Missenden (012406 8818); Peter Wylie, Plymtree Manor, Cullompton, Devon (018847 555); and T & W, 51 King Street, Thetford, Norfolk (01842 76546).

April 21, 1990

AUSTRALIA'S USER-FRIENDLY WINE EXPERT

James Halliday is a 51-year-old lawyer turned author, columnist, wine judge and wine producer who seems to have discovered the secret of eternal activity. He was in London last week in connection with two of the 13 books which in 12 months he will either have had published, completed or agreed to write or co-write.

It presumably helps to have a wife as driven and energetic as he is, and it is Suzanne Halliday who is minding the vats full of a particularly successful 1990 vintage back at their Coldstream Hills winery in Victoria's trendy (since Halliday moved there) Yarra Valley while James snoops around France this week.

I tracked him down at a wine tasting in London NW1 where he was busy lecturing the foremost wine writers of Britain on the difference between brettanomyces (the new cult wine fault), corkiness and the role played by chlorine in both. Not that he'd been invited to deliver a lecture - but being 6ft 3in tall, long on decibels and practical experience, he just can't help it.

Over lunch - "Look, let me do the wine" - he couldn't help ruminating about the effects of Australia's recession on its burgeoning wine industry, which should mean lots of cheap(ish) wine for us. There's a serious cash flow problem and, in the wake of this year's merger of the two biggest companies Penfolds and Lindemans, apparently lunatic discounting is rife.

Lindemans' Nyrang Hermitage (the Australian wine industry has long made free with the names of the European wines it affects to despise) was Halliday's "wine of the week" in *The Australian* earlier this year at A$3.99. What is true for finished wine is true for the raw ingredients. Two years ago the spot price of a tonne of Chardonnay grapes at the end of the harvest was as high as A$2,200. This year it was A$800, and a significant proportion of the 1990 vintage, another bumper crop, was left unpicked. A parcel of precious Yarra Pinot

Noir, admittedly from "a crook vineyard", was sold only with the greatest difficulty at A$400 a tonne.

Quite apart from the pressures of cash flow and having the market quite so dominated by one company - as in California with Gallo - there is Australian wine's unfamiliar problem of a falling domestic market exacerbated by slowing exports. "It simply had to happen," said Halliday over the foie gras. "The 100 per cent growth of recent years was unsustainable. The US has been pretty much a disaster and probably always will be for all but a few large Australian wine companies.

"We're competing with California which is a very viable, vibrant industry that's much more effective, and much bigger, than the Australian one. [I was to learn that he feels strongly about California.] No, our obvious export markets have to be the UK, Scandinavia and Japan". Halliday believes that before too long Japan will be the prime export market for Australian wine but that approval in Britain and France will play a vital, if reflexive, role - London for "the mirror effect" ie, Japan will overbid the Brits for the wines the Brits obviously want; France for the "reflected glory" that accrues to any wine industry in which the French are themselves so keen to invest.

"I don't have any hang-ups about the French in Australia at all." He is proud that so many French, mainly Champagne, companies have taken a stake in his native wine industry - indeed his own eyrie-like winery looks down on Moët & Chandon's eye-catching Australian sparkling wine production centre. According to Halliday, Christian Moueix of Pomerol first questioned him keenly about investment in the Yarra in 1982, and he is also awaiting with interest some concrete result from a grand tour of Australia made by Vincent Leflaive, king of Puligny-Montrachet, two years ago.

"I want more outside investment not less. I don't think the French can teach us much about making wine in Australia," he said robustly, "even if they could teach us a bit about viticulture. Most of Australia's winemakers are aware of the French techniques but they're not that keen to use them. If you're on a winning streak, why change?"

What he means is that Australia has profited from producing notably obvious user-friendly wines geared to the outside world, as opposed to France's more introspective, more structured, longer-living specimens.

"We put the emphasis on fruit flavour," he said happily. "Unlike the Californians, we don't have this obsession with complexity, or making wines to go with food. I think the Americans have so sensitised their palates - all this no-salt stuff - that they've ended up producing decaffeinated everything, including wine. I really think they've made the most terrible mistake..."

The irony of course is that at Coldstream Hills, Halliday is aiming precisely for complexity and development potential but this he brushes aside with a mutter about niche markets. I pressed him for some specific winemaking differences between France and Australia.

"Well, the French don't care about the degree of juice oxidation; they leave the juice much cloudier; their use of sulphur dioxide is decidedly erratic (fellow customers turned as he enunciated that penultimate syllable); they ferment at much higher temperatures; and, except in the great estates, the French use much less new oak."

But how can the Australians, whose wine prices are so low, afford the luxury of new French oak casks, I wondered. "Ah well," said Halliday, "there is no question that the big companies in Australia use an awful lot of oak chips. It's perfectly legal, in fact the very people who sell the barrels in Australia also peddle the oak chips." Careful label study is needed. There may be the world of difference between a wine that is "oak-aged" and one that has "spent months in new Nevers oak puncheons."

As we pushed away the remains of our pigeon, virtuously refused another course and ostentatiously left a third of a bottle of the Volnay 1986 from Blain-Gagnard - our admiration for his white wines intact - I felt I had to quiz him about one of the great idiosyncrasies of Australia's wine industry - the show system of marathon judgings and medals.

How many wines did he judge in a day at a show? "200. No, look, 180. 140 is a slack day." And did he never have qualms about giving the last wine as good a go as the first? "No, I'd never make that sort of statement. It really depends on how you feel that day, but do remember that we work our way through different classes, from light whites through to the stickies; they're not all the same sort of wines.

"It was an absolute nightmare once when I had to do 200 Rhine Rieslings. It really was awfully embarrassing feeling as lost as I did. My record is 285 - different classes - in a single day. Where? I knew you'd ask me that. Now where was it? Could've been Ballarat last year. I'm just not sure. I seem to have done an awful lot of judging recently."

I asked who was going to inherit the mantle of Australia's most famous wine man, Len Evans, chairman of judges at the national wine show and several others. "Who's going to take over from Len? God knows." He looked at me sideways and we both smiled. "Well, I suppose it could be me."

SOME HALLIDAY FAVOURITES

Houghton's White Supreme. The best-selling Houghton's White Burgundy down under. Older vintages demonstrate that this blend of unusual varieties from the oft despised Swan Valley in Western Australia is a cracker. Full-bodied, tangy and deeply individual. £4.55 Waitrose.

Basedows Wood-aged Semillon 1988. Halliday has great respect for winemaker Doug Lehmann (son of crag-faced Peter) and his way with whites in particular. This one, from an excellent vintage, is £5.95 from Adnams of Southwold.

Basedows Semillon and Chardonnay 1989 are £5.98 and £6.98 respectively from Bibendum of London NW1. Other Basedows stockists include Goedhuis & Co of London SW11 and Oxford and Cambridge Fine Wine of Cambridge.

Other more expensive producers to receive Halliday's seal of approval include, in the order he mentioned them, Petaluma, Henschke, Bannockburn, Goundrey, Wignalls, Cape Mentelle, Moss Wood and Pipers Brook.

May 19, 1990

Leflaive have shown no inclination to invest in Australia. The traditional method sparkling wine made by Moët next door to Halliday's Coldstream Hills has been selling well under the Green Point label. Halliday continues to write several books a year.

... the introduction of oak chips....

DRINKING IN THE RAIN

Two weeks ago today I went to a lunch party in the Minervois, way down south in France's most concentrated vine-growing countryside. The men were in shorts, the women in sun dresses. Everyone under 20 had brought a swimsuit. Guests eyed the pool as they sipped their vin blanc cassis before going inside for the shade the French always seek for the serious business of eating.

By 4.30, as three whole roast sheep were making their impact on several score stomachs, we were trapped inside by a downpour of almost tropical force. In half an hour alone more than 40mm (11 or 12 inches) of rain fell - twice the average for the whole of July in this arid region. The rain drops ricocheted off the tiles round a swimming pool that was rising by the minute. The hundreds of valleys between the curved Midi roof tiles above us spurted a crystal bead curtain of impenetrable waterfalls. We were marooned from the coffee that had been brewing in the house next door.

In English the word "dampen" is strictly pejorative. The hostess whose summer party ends with a cloudburst is encouraged by commiseration to feel a sense of failure. The French know no such association between water and low spirits. The verb *arroser*, meaning "to water, to wet," has such positive associations that it can also mean to toast or celebrate.

Instead of long faces at the onset of this rainstorm our fellow lunch guests ran to the windows and whooped with joy. Our hosts beamed with pride at this unexpected entertainment. *"C'est super!"* they kept exclaiming to each other as they watched the surrounding vineyards being washed downhill. One particular pragmatic vine grower nodded at the liquid heavens, *"Bouteilles! Bouteilles!"* (Bottles! Bottles!) he beamed.

Yes, after three years of dangerous drought, with *la secheresse* a regular feature of the *Midi Libre* reportage, the vine growers of this little bit of the Languedoc-Roussillon at least were being palpably rewarded with bottles of extra wine thanks to this rare downpour. In the whole of May, June and July the previous year they had seen only a sixth as much rain as fell that afternoon.

It was as we watched the rainclouds blowing in over the vineyards from the south-westernmost foothills of the Massif Central that one of the vignerons reminded us there was nothing new in the region's water shortage. He had been dismantling some concrete vats built by this grandfather - a common task in the region at the moment, often undertaken by dynamite, to make way for flashy new stainless steel (although up in Bordeaux Château Pétrus sticks to concrete). A complete cross section revealed the concrete a pretty pink through and through. Water must have been so scarce that his grandfather had used wine, of which the region has never been short, to mix the cement.

We tend to view wine as an alternative to water, forgetting that water is not just an essential prerequisite for wine production, it is what wine is made of, constituting well over three-quarters of the volume. Grape juice, and therefore wine, exists initially as water in the soil, drawn up through a vine's roots to plump out its fruit. Although the vine's ability to establish a particularly deep root system means that it can survive rainfall too low to sustain most agricultural crops (other than olives) the plant, like any other, must have some water to promote growth and swell the all-important fruit.

The more water the plant absorbs during the growing season, the juicier the fruit will be and the greater the eventual volume of wine produced - which usually means, as our Minervois friends well know, more income for the producer. If there is too much rain, as in some German, English, Bordeaux and Burgundy vintages, the grapes tend to lack fermentable sugar and flavouring elements and can be weak, thin little things.

If a vine doesn't get enough water, it behaves like so many plants in British gardens have been doing this summer and wilts, so overcome by the drought that it simply stops work. In vines this severe moisture stress, a regular feature of some California and Australian vineyards, brings the grape ripening process to a grinding halt. This can result in wines with such a high ration of solids to juice that they are unpleasantly, or at least inconveniently, dry and tannic - as the 1976 red burgundies or many 1980 north California reds were, for instance.

Bordeaux has just suffered exceptionally high temperatures for the third year running. If the global warming forecasters are right, wine regions whose regulations and practices are based on their being temperate are going to become hotter and drier. Burgundy's most cosmopolitan ambassador, Robert Drouhin, admits that he took the greenhouse effect into account when siting his new Oregon vineyard, planting in a higher, cooler site than would have made sense 10 years ago. New World vine growers have long used technology to compensate for natural disadvantages, irrigation being the most obvious example. Unlike European producers they have no inhibitions or laws to stop them giving stressed vines as much moisture as they require and, in some instances, more. If you have ever wondered why a cheap Australian or California wine tastes of so little, it is probably because it has been made from vines that have been over-enthusiastically irrigated - bulk without hulk.

It is partly because irrigation is so obviously a potentially dangerous instrument in wine production that officialdom in the classical wine regions is so wary of it. Even the poor Central Spaniards whose rainfall is as low as much of North Africa's are not allowed a single man-made trickle, which keeps their average output per acre at a far lower level than that of northern Europe.

But methods of irrigation have become much more sophisticated. Quality-conscious wine producers can dramatically improve their vintage by a few well-judged drops from a drip irrigation system, knowing that flooding or indiscriminate sprinkling of the vineyard will mean more, but punier wine.

Major changes in climate may mean the authorities have to rethink their attitude to irrigation - especially now that the wine market is driven by quality rather than quantity. Down in the Languedoc, vineyards can be irrigated - but not those destined to produce the superior (but only just higher priced) Appellation Contrôlée wine. Since most producers make both AC wines and Vins de Pays, how on earth do the authorities control irrigation, I asked a local official. "Ha!" was the reply.

But a good downpour can do more than a drip. As Guy Bascou, one of the most influential winemaking consultants in the Languedoc tried to point out at our lunch party (to a shopkeeper from Paris who was confidently telling him otherwise), a really good shower usefully washes the dust off the leaves and helps the sturdy vine get back to work. I remember being told by the Californian manager of the Napa Valley vineyard part-owned by Christian Moueix of Château Pétrus that Moueix had specifically instructed him to sluice the vineyard dust off the vines each summer.

Nowadays water is needed every bit as much in the cellar as in the vineyard. As temperatures have risen, and consumers have learnt to scorn obviously "hot" or oxidised wines, winemakers have to be able to cool their cellars and, in particular, fermentation vats. This most commonly involves trickling icy water down their outsides or enveloping them in a jacket of ice. And then when the winemaking is over, gallons and gallons of water are needed to hose down all the hoppers, presses and tanks of modern winemaking. Hygiene is something only the well-watered can afford.

Although there are still exceptions - anachronistic and gloriously successful *caves* such as the flyblown, fetid old byres of Château Rayas in Châteauneuf-du-Pape where there is probably a lone, dubious tap - the modern winery demands a generous and reliable water source, as the magnificently isolated California hilltop wineries of Calera and Chalone have found to their cost.

And of course there is one final way in which water is an invaluable adjunct to wine. All of us who drink wine know that it is a poor thirst quencher. A glass of good water is needed alongside. I asked Henri Krug of the famous Champagne house the other day what he drinks at home. He admitted to not a bad house wine but added "and water too. In this trade water is very important indeed." And never more so.

August 8, 1990

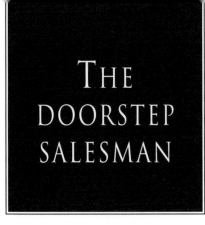

THE DOORSTEP SALESMAN

I f you believe the patter of its sales staff, the world's largest shipper of wine is a company called Vicomte Bernard de Romanet. I have a cheery sales leaflet in front of me signed "Regards, B de Romanet" who seems to be based at The International Wine Centre in - where else? - Dallow Road, Luton. Only the telex address, PIER, hints at the company's parent, the German direct sales specialist Pieroth, not a name to impress those of us who studied the Austro-German diethylene glycol scandal of 1985 in any detail and one that was recently successfully prosecuted for selling £22,000 worth of under-strength English wine.

"The reason that not a lot of people have heard of us," explained one of the nobleman's 75 UK salesmen as he shook out various dinky little napkin-cum-tablecloths to protect my table from wine stains, "is because we like to keep the service personal. The way we like to do business is through recommendations and suchlike."

My own recommendation came from a computer salesman who heard me complain I couldn't find a bottle of the delicious Château Clerc-Milon 1986 the length and breadth of Britain. "Pierre Laforest, Dallow Road, Luton" he'd kindly scribbled on the back of his card. (I know not how Pierre is related to Bernard but suspect Pierre Laforest is the name of yet another Pieroth subsidiary.)

The next thing I knew, a matey male voice was trying to convince me by telephone that 1987 Clerc-Milon was "almost identical" to Clerc-Milon 1986 ("because Baron de Rothschild wouldn't put his name on the label if it wasn't"). Curious to find out more about an outfit that so brazenly conflated two of Bordeaux's most dissimilar vintages, I accepted his offer to let me taste the Vicomte's wares chez moi, which is how I came to be marvelling at his sales kit of bottles, complete with ice pack in summer and pink rubber hot water bottle in winter.

"All the wines you're about to taste are solely exclusive to Romanet. You won't find them in any off-licence," he assured me. "We actually own the vineyard, process the wine and ship it over to our bonded warehouse in Luton." And where is this the vineyard? "Everywhere", he boasted. "All over France, Germany, the US, Hong Kong, everywhere." Hong Kong? Surely some mistake in the Viscount's training manual here.

I asked him about the two thimble-sized, machine-hewn wine-glasses he reverentially unwrapped from a tea towel. "I don't like to use plastic tasting cups," he told me fastidiously. "I think that wines of this quality deserve to go into a glass, so I don't mind spending out on glasses."

Keen to distance his company from the wine-retailing rat-race he said sniffily, "Sainsbury's and Tesco cover the bottom end of the market and we're not really interested in that level. We are purveyors of fine wines. I can't guarantee you're going to enjoy the wines. What I can guarantee is their quality." The message, it would seem, is that if you don't like them, it's because your palate isn't sufficiently well-trained. But stick with the Vicomte - and his free, indoctrinating, intoxicating samples - and you'll have something superior, sales pitch included, that none of the neighbours will have access to.

I tasted nine French wines, from Cuvée des Ondines 1989, a rather flat white Côtes du Roussillon ("from the Languedoc region") at £4.85, to a 1987 red Châteauneuf-du-Pape at £13.95. My overriding impression had nothing to do with quality, which was absolutely average, but price, which was way, way, way above average. (Sainsbury's charge £2.49 for their red Côtes du Roussillon, usually far better than the white, and £6.95 for their very respectable red Châteauneuf.)

Pieroth's policy has always been to cover themselves from direct comparison by using names and labels exclusive to them, most of them in this case (and they run several companies in tandem with the Vicomte's) signalling that the wine has been bottled in St Jean d'Ardières, a small town on the N6 north of Lyons as it skims the Beaujolais region. My salesman's claim that "our actual headquarters is in the heart of the Burgundy region" suggests that his promised educational trip to France will come not a moment too soon.

The Vicomte's vintages could hardly be younger (and therefore less costly on the internal French wine market) either. His generic red bordeaux, the sort of wine you can pick up for under £2.50 if you choose to shop from a shelf, is a 1989. It carries a fancy name, Les Beaux Monts, and the brazen price tag of £6.29. "That one's drinking quite well at the moment", I was assured before we moved on to a St Emilion from that dubious vintage 1987, "one of the 1944 classification wines". (I think he meant the 1955 classification, revised and renamed twice since but never to elevate the Vicomte's mysterious chosen property, Château Tour de Cauze, unlisted in the Bordeaux bible Féret, above yeoman rank.)

The wine that called for the most arresting sales line however was the last, the Châteauneuf, Château de la Gardine 1987 (at £13.95 a good fiver above even the market leader) which came in one of those artfully-deformed bottles found in less quality-conscious Italian delicatessens. "Yup, that's gotta lotta history to it," the salesman told me triumphantly. "This particular wine actually dates back to the 1300s when the Pope of the time in Avignon, who was actually in charge of the vineyards, was arthritic and they designed this bottle so he could grip it. See? And that's no sales pitch. It's all on the back label and every bottle's numbered and registered and so forth.

"And the white Châteauneuf's really special. Only 1.8 per cent white wine is made in the region but the Gardine white is really superb. It's £17.95." Sacre bleu! Can it really be as good as Beaucastel's very special bottling from ancient Roussanne vines (£17.65 from Adnams of Southwold and one of the few white Châteauneufs I'd ever choose to buy)?

There was worse to come when he reluctantly handed me a price list. ("It's just our worksheet really. It can't tell you about the wines like tasting them does.") To my horror I saw that prices did not include VAT, or a £3 delivery charge, and that the minimum order was a bizarre 18 bottles, when even wholesale licensing laws never stipulate more than 12.

He squirmed a bit as he explained this greedy idiosyncrasy. Presumably this question comes up pretty regularly with the "builders, bankers, doctors, solicitors, lawyers - anybody really who enjoys fine wine", as he describes his customers. "What we have is a bonded warehouse where it comes in by the case and so by legal terms we have to sell by the case. What happens is, the cases come in three packs of six which are all stuck together, making 18 bottles, which we call a case. But what we can do is cut the cases so that we can sell you six bottles of three different wines." So kind.

He gallantly allowed me a few days to think about it and, as he rolled up his napkins again and rinsed his minuscule glasses, hauled out some of the unused patter. I was invited to shake my head in horror with him at the rapacious pricing policy of some restaurants. "I was in a restaurant last night and they were asking over £10 for an ordinary Mâcon. I couldn't believe it. (Our Mâcon-Villages is £7.99.)

"What happens is, once you've actually bought some of Ramonet's wines, what we like to say is that you've joined the company. Then you get invites to boat trips, wine tastings and suchforth. We just had one at the Tower Thistle - all good fun. And then you get the opportunity to buy wine at reduced rates; free gifts come through the post like cheeseboards, little things like that. We're not just a company that sells wine, we like to pride ourselves on the way we treat our customers."

He was really too nice for this game, having drifted into it after a few years as wine waiter who had to work over Christmas. I felt sorry for him. I relented after his follow-up telephone call, easily talked him down from his 18-bottle minimum and ended up spending £110 on a dozen bottles of wines I don't need and whose exact like I know I can buy at the half the price elsewhere. But at least I *knew* I was paying over the odds.

February 2, 1991

WHAT'S SPECIAL ABOUT ALSACE

Being female has caused me only one problem as a wine writer, but I consider it a serious one. I happened to be in Alsace during the most delicate stage of my first pregnancy and for years afterwards couldn't lift a glass of the region's distinctively perfumed wine to my lips without feeling queasy.

But now that our firstborn is old enough to describe most of her parents' actions as "gross", the spell seems to be broken. I have fallen in love again with the wines of Alsace and have been seizing every opportunity to renew my acquaintance with smoky dry whites that make unusually good aperitifs (far better than Chardonnay) as well having the guts to stand up to foods as variously powerful as venison, Vacherin and Vindaloo.

The thing people tell you about these wines is that Alsace winemakers are so consistent it's impossible to find a disappointing bottle. Don't believe a word of it. Some of my recent purchases, especially of Rieslings, have been as dull, and sometimes as dirty, as ditchwater.

But when they are good, Alsace wines are very, very good and, as elsewhere, we have the blue chip 1988, luscious 1989 and hyperrich 1990 vintages to choose from. Other good recent vintages are 1983, 1985 and, more variable, 1986 but, as in Burgundy, the producer is the vital factor.

Also as in Burgundy, there is increasing polarisation of producers. On the one hand are the large (by Alsace standards) negociants such as Hugel, Trimbach, Beyer and the Dopffs who buy in grapes from other growers and blend wines to sell under their own special labels. Their top bottlings are some of the very finest wines of the region.

HUGEL has for years been showing the rest how to make the extraordinary late harvest wines labelled Vendange Tardive and, even sweeter, Sélection de Grains Nobles. In the more usual dry-but-perfumed style of Alsace however, I have found that to be sure of real excitement behind a Hugel label, you have to buy their top range, once called Réserve Personnelle, now called Jubilee (available from OW Loeb, London SE1 about £120 a case; La Vigneronne of London SW7 have halves of Riesling 1985 for £6.95).

TRIMBACH, more famous in the US, is terrific at slow-maturing steely Rieslings such as their Clos Ste Hune and Cuvée Frederic Emile, while LEON BEYER is the king of Gewurztraminer making extraordinarily opulent wines, particularly those labelled Cuvée des Comtes d'Eguisheim.

But the monopoly that the large houses enjoyed in export markets has been broken, just as in Burgundy, by individual domaines. Growers who bottle the produce of their own vineyards now export more than four times as much wine as they did in 1980, while total exports have grown by a half.

And the best of these growers is singing the sort of tune that today's more sophisticated wine drinker wants to hear. It goes t-e-r-r-o-i-r. Rather than blending wine to match their own special labels, effectively brand names, the likes of Zind-Humbrecht, Marcel Deiss, André Ostertag and Paul Blanck are dedicated to expressing the particular conditions of a single terrain, one carefully delineated vineyard, and usually one that qualifies as a Grand Cru.

Alsace's superior Grand Cru appellation had a difficult birth back in 1975 and is still in intensive care. The negociants are quite right that the words Grand Cru on a label are no guarantee of quality. On the other hand, a Grand Cru from one of the new generation of geography-conscious growers will probably be one of the more thrilling wines you will ever taste, full of searing fruit and intense aroma.

ZIND-HUMBRECHT may be one of the most expensive Alsace producers but the premium is well-deserved; you can taste the concentration of low-yield vines in the glass. The current bargain has to be their straight Riesling 1989 (£6.99 from Wine Rack) which is far better than many Grand Cru Rieslings I have tasted recently. And unlike most of the Zind-Humbrecht wines that Thresher and Wine Rack shops have been clever enough to snap up, this rich-yet-dry wine is ready to drink.

Any Zind-Humbrecht wine, and Thresher and Wine Rack have a good selection, is worth trying but the current star is the super-potent dry Gewurztraminer Clos Windsbuhl 1989 (£14.95 from Wine Rack) and, for the really long term, Riesling Clos Hauserer 1988 (£8.49 Thresher and Wine Rack).

MARCEL DEISS exhibits even more fanaticism in his devotion to the notion of terroir and Grands Crus. Lea & Sandeman of London SW10 have a wide selection, from a 1989 Sylvaner at £4.85 to a quite extraordinary Riesling 1988 Grand Cru Schoenenberg, Sélection de Grains Nobles that constitutes essence of Riesling, as well it might at £39.95 a bottle.

ANDRE OSTERTAG is another young Turk of the region who has been tinkering away like mad with the old formulae. His 'vins de fruit' are designed to show off the grape, his 'vins de pierre' the terroir. He has also been experimenting with deliberate oak ageing, even for Pinot Blanc. His wines can be bought relatively reasonably by the case from Morris & Verdin of London SW1 or by the bottle from La Vigneronne, SW7 or Wines of Paris in Edinburgh.

Philippe BLANCK also has the slightly eerie glint of a fanatic. The excellent wines of his family firm Paul Blanck are available, in their dramatically non-Alsatian bottles and labels, from Adnams of Southwold. Their Pinot Blanc 1989 is a good buy at £4.40 but the Riesling 1988 Grand Cru Furstentum has more potential for purists than one might expect for £8.70.

Another reliable and quite widely distributed name is a good one, ROLLY-GASSMAN, whose sweeter-than-most wines are sold by Bibendum of London NW1 (some 1983s still available), Thos Peatling of Bury St Edmunds, Tanners of Shrewsbury and Raeburn Fine Wines of Edinburgh.

But perhaps my favourite producer of all is THEO FALLER of the DOMAINE WEINBACH (both names are used on wine lists). OW Loeb of London SE1 import these as well as Hugel wines, but Lay & Wheeler of Colchester can offer Faller's Riesling 1988 Grand Cru Schlossberg by the bottle for a fully justified £10.70. (They also have the wines of SCHLUMBERGER which can be delicious.)

Another old Alsace saw is that the co-ops here are brilliant. That's not universally true either but the TURCKHEIM CO-OP is excellent and its well-made wines, even including some Grand Cru wines such as their almost painfully dense Tokay Pinot Gris 1989 Brand (£8.99 Thresher and Wine Rack), are widely distributed and well priced.

Alsace inamoratae like me are best served by Thresher, Wine Rack and La Vigneronne.

July 13, 1991

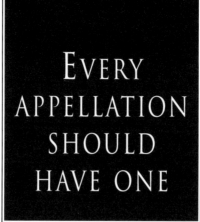

EVERY APPELLATION SHOULD HAVE ONE

Robert Plageoles should have his own television show. A late night arts discussion programme preferably, all abstract nouns and shrugs. Instead of which he has to expound from an almost embarrassingly modest farmhouse perched on top of one of the rolling green hills of Gaillac, an obscure appellation in the south-west of France. Thanks to Plageoles, it is fast losing its obscurity. In fact the only reason that news of Gaillac's renaissance has been slow to spread to the English-speaking world, where we still think Gaillac produces nothing but nondescript co-operative pop, is that Plageoles speaks only French.

As he so rightly says, "I know how to talk about wine, and French is the language best suited to talking about wine the way I do."

Let me give you an example of the Plageoles way with wine and words. After half an hour of verbal assault - during which he had given me a dazzling exposition on Cathar drinking habits, ancient Languedoc place names, the role of collective memory and the extent to which local vine varieties must be saved from extinction, all the time rotating his shoulders and hands on at least 20 different axes and flashing his impressive gold dentalwork - I asked him whether he felt his very distinctive style of wine (frank, direct, full of flavour) owed more to the vineyard or the cellar.

He put his pen to his lips and nodded slowly before giving a reply that was very Plageoles, very different from the usual techno-talk. "That's an interesting question. What indeed is wine?" At this point my notes in English of what he said in French betray my lack of professionalism. Make what you will of: "Wine is part of our patrimony. What's important is the spirit in which it is vinified. When one makes wine, one brings a reflection of a soul. I'm trying to restore to Mauzac [one of his beloved native vines of Gaillac] its veritable identity which is multiform." Et cetera.

The people of Gaillac (other than his most irritated competitors) are proud of their articulate archivist, a spokesman who has earned their appellation so many column inches in the French press. The sommeliers of nearby Albi look touchingly grateful when you mention Robert Plageoles, and when we asked the way to him of an archetypal little old lady in his nearest village, her verbatim response was "Ooh la la!".

With his handsome features, curly locks, snappy sweater and blouson marked 'Chino Lifestyle' across still athletic shoulders he belies his 56 years and looks distinctly Hollywood - at any rate far too big for his small desk and struggling appellation. But it is clearly the struggle he relishes. His return to the small family wine farm in 1981 followed 28 years of trade union work and now he is fighting for a better deal for the wines of Gaillac.

In the Middle Ages Gaillac wines were some of the most sought after and the Bordeaux trade had to play all manner of tricks to stave off competition from them. Recently however the appellation has been too diffuse and too dull to win many friends. Gaillac could be sparkling or still; sweet or dry; red, white or pink; ordinary or downright poor. At least such were the wines, almost all of them local varieties blended with more familiar 'international' ones, that were exported from the region.

But now there is a new sense of dynamism and pride in Gaillac that is evident in top bottlings from the likes of Domaine d'Escausses. It cannot be dissociated from Plageoles' notably médiatique activities, particularly the revival of ancient grape varieties and wine styles. "I've started a little revolution", he admits of his policy of bottling each grape variety separately. "There is a message of truth in a vine variety. A varietal wine is a naked wine. You cannot hide faults. My motivation is that I am saving our local heritage. It has been an enriching experience for me."

He probably does not mean by this that Plageoles wines, ten different sorts from a mere 25 hectares of vines, command an impressive premium over other Gaillacs. The cellar-door price of his beloved Mauzac Nature - an appley, naturally fizzy, defiantly cloudy young white from a Gaillac variety also important in Blanquette de Limoux - is by local standards wildly expensive at 34 francs (£3.40). His sleek, unusually fruity red Duras (a local vine variety rather than the place 100 miles north-west) is 27 francs (£2.70) a bottle. And his really special wines such as his sherry-like 'Vin de Voile' and 'Vin d'Autan', a sweet white made from almost-extinct Ondenc vines, command prices as high as 300 francs (£30) a bottle. (These cleverly registered names give him valuable exclusivity.)

I bought a mixed case of these beautifully labelled wines that was to completely and deliciously revive my faith in Gaillac. Ironically it was the despised 'outsider' varieties Sauvignon and Gamay that were particularly impressive.

As 35 year-old Bernard, the hands-on Plageoles, packaged the bottles, his father, still holding forth, rummaged in an old cardboard box to show me some of the dusty volumes on which his wine and vine research was based and then, ignoring the screams of my baby, would not let me go until he had pressed into my hand his document on exact serving temperatures for each one of his wines. Dedication indeed.

Outside France the wines of Robert Plageoles (Tel. 63.33.90.40.) are rarely seen but he has sent small quantities to Germany, Switzerland, Canada, Le Montrachet restaurant in New York and Le Perignon in Tokyo.

August 10, 1991

WINE SPELT WITH TWO SEAS

I f you were to take the tree-lined Route Nationale 113 from Bordeaux, centre of the traditional wine world, to the unrivalled concentration of wine bargains that is today's Languedoc, the first vineyards you would come to, after three or four hours bisecting vast sweeps of cereals and sunflowers, would be those of Cabardès (pron. 'Cab-are-dess').

Here the scale is altogether different. Narrow roads, heady with the Mediterranean scents of wild fennel and thyme, dip and dive around patches of vines punctuated by garrigue and pines. White boulders and rocky outcrops are the more obvious manifestations of geological diversity. From them you can see the extraordinary turreted Cité of Carcassonne just to the south and, on a clear day, west along the Pyrenees all the way to Lourdes.

It looks idyllic and the two dozen wine producers of Cabardès are dedicated to keeping it so, but they have a problem. Their export prices are often as low as 8 francs, or 80p, per smart ex-château bottle.

What brings headaches and near-penury to these vignerons and thousands of others in the Languedoc-Roussillon is of course a gift, literally, to wine consumers. But the unusually cohesive, committed and uncomplaining band of Cabardès producers can offer those used to the flavours and dimensions of red bordeaux something special: an introduction to the Languedoc that is not just geographical but tasteable. Cabardès, almost all of it red, tastes like a halfway house between the familiar Cabernets and Merlots of Bordeaux's Atlantic vineyards and the Languedoc's more Mediterranean make-up of Grenache, Syrah, Cinsaut and the ubiquitous Carignan vine.

A full-blooded St Chinian or Fitou can come as a bit of a meridional shock to a palate reared on St Estèphe or even Fronsac, but a typical Cabardès has the same sort of weight as a bordeaux and contains a cocktail of 'atlantic' and 'mediterranean' grape varieties.

Cabardès is still only a VDQS wine and therefore a bit of a squit in French eyes vis-à-vis those that have already earned full AC status, but the Appellation Contrôlée authorities are already inspecting every pebble of Cabardès' three or four hundred hectares of vineyard with a view to promotion.

The producers would like to see in the AC rulebook a maximum of 60 per cent of Cabernet Sauvignon, Cabernet Franc, Merlot, Cot (Malbec) and the weird and wonderful Fer Servadou of Marcillac and a minimum of 40 per cent of Syrah, Grenache, Cinsaut (mainly for rose) and Carignan (which is fast being replaced by more respectable varieties).

As Gabriel Tari, a young lawyer who decided to dedicate himself to upgrading his family's Château de Brau says defiantly, "We don't want to be like the rest of the world making just another wine that tastes like Bordeaux".

His property is in the south-eastern sector of the region where, as one would expect, the mediterranean varieties predominate and the wines, such as those of garlanded Château Salitis, taste rounder, riper and fuller as a result.

Another of the region's bigger properties, and probably the most widely available, is the historic Château de Pennautier ("Molière stayed here"), whose holdings include vineyards spread widely over Cabardès' varied subregions. Château de Pennautier 1987 is just £2.90 at Sainsbury's and the much riper 1989 is £3.49 at Peatlings, London EC1 and East Anglia and £3.45 at Haynes Hanson and Clark of SW6. These very Cabernet wines are also shipped from this tiny vine outpost to San Francisco.

Patrons of Britain's Majestic Wine Warehouses may well be familiar with the wines of Chateau de Ventenac whose 1989, the red of which the skilful owner Alain Maurel is most proud, is £2.99. Waitrose sell his Domaine Leclaud Cabernet 1989 for £2.95 - a much better buy than the muddy, blended Cabardès Waitrose stock at £2.79. The more acid soils of Ventenac on the west, more atlantic side of the region make for distinctive reds and delicate roses that express well the unique 'Vin de Deux Mers' style of Cabardès.

The region has been paid the compliment of relatively new investment. A talented young winemaker from the Conques co-operative will be making his own first vintage at La Ventaiolle this year and Domaine des Caunettes-Hautes, also in the west, is the result of hard work on the part of the Rouquet brothers previously in the cereal business. Their attractively Syrah-influenced 1989 is £3.49 at Unwins. Eaton Elliott of Alderley Edge have the robust Château Rivals 1988.

On the other side of Carcassonne is another VDQS candidate for AC status and the appellation Ideal Introduction to the Languedoc, Cotes de la Malepère. Prices are equally attractive but the region, being wetter and more westerly, is even more atlantic-influenced and, with the exception of such dedicated individuals as Henri Turetti at the Domaine de Matibat, tends to be much more dominated by big co-operatives than the more individualistic Cabardès to the north.

As the age of vines in the newly renovated vineyards of Cabardès increases, and as winemaking expertise and equipment improve (Fullers are currently selling off an out-of-condition Cabardès at £1.33; destalkers and oak barrels are rarities), the wines of Cabardès should get better and better. They are already beautifully packaged, looking at first glance almost indistinguishable from a chateau bottled claret costing three times the price. In fact one wonders how many wine buyers have picked a bottle off the shelf thinking that Cabardès is that famous red grape variety they use in Bordeaux.

September 14, 1991

VIOGNIER - A-LEVEL GEWURZTRAMINER

According to top London restaurateur Nico Ladenis, Condrieu is the one wine he can sell more easily than he can buy. Once tasted, or at least sniffed, this exotic white is certainly difficult to forget, like the headily distinctive Gewurztraminer of Alsace that has in its time turned many a neophyte on to wine. Full-bodied yet dry, with a unique scent reminding some of apricots, others of may blossom and musk, Condrieu is a sort of Chardonnay with knobs on.

There is only one problem with Condrieu. A good one can easily cost £20 a bottle, because the total vineyard area on steep, difficult-to-cultivate slopes above the Rhône south of Lyons is so small. It is, once more, on the increase but is still only 40 hectares (88 acres). Local vignerons complain of the unreliability of the very special Viognier (pron. "Vee-on-yeh") grape to which Condrieu owes its perfume. The vine's average yield of around 20 hectolitres per hectare is hardly economically viable. This leaves only a few thousand cases of Condrieu a year to satisfy all the restaurants, and retailers, of the world. Not nearly enough.

Help is at hand however. Cuttings of Viognier are being disseminated around the world and it is now possible to buy wines labelled Viognier, some of them tasting remarkably like Condrieu, from regions as far apart as California's obscure San Benito County and Corbières.

Jacques Boyer is an agricultural merchant specialising in selling decidedly unfashionable chemicals (supplemented increasingly by more modish biologically-based alternatives) based in the village of Homps in the lower reaches of the Minervois appellation. Like most of his neighbours, he inherited a few hectares of vineyard which, like those of most of his neighbours, were planted with undistinguished Carignan vines whose lacklustre produce is tipped straight into the local co-operative.

One day his eye strayed from the crossword puzzle he was doing in his wife's *Femme Actuelle* to a paragraph outlining Condrieu's rarity and very special characteristics. He bought a bottle in 1987 and by April 1988 had grafted Viognier cuttings collected from Georges Vernay, one of the most respected producers of Condrieu, on to one hectare (2.2 acres) of his 10 year-old Carignan vine trunks - a technique that has helped California growers keep pace with fluctuations in fashion there without having to wait the three years necessary for vines grown from scratch. His father thought he was he mad.

His first vintage was 1989. It was quite delicious and had a lovely pure Viognier aroma for the first year of its life. He asked 45 francs (£4.50) for a bottle of this humbly ranked Vin de Pays de l'Aude (Viognier is not a variety officially sanctioned by the Appellation Contrôlée laws for Minervois). His neighbours, who might get 15 francs for a bottle of white Minervois with full AC status, also thought he was mad, but he sold every bottle.

This year, now that he is asking 60 francs for a much denser, more long-lasting (though variable) 1990 Viognier, they think he is merely criminal. But when I visited in August he was allocating, not selling, cases to the top local restaurateurs and had just been visited by a particularly fashion-conscious American importer.

Also in Minervois, some rich, almost heavy Viognier was made in 1990 at La Combe Blanche above La Livinière and Roger Piquet is equally taken with his third year Viognier at Château de Gourgazaud which has borne fruit for the first time this year.

Viognier-planting seems to be one of the most popular sports in the Languedoc at the moment, where 16 hectares of the variety are already officially recorded but this is almost certainly an underestimate.

The large firm of Skalli has managed to find 2000 litres to ferment in smart barrels in their spage-age winery in Sète this year. Other properties boasting a few hectares of modish Viognier vines include Etang de Colombes in Corbières, and an increasing number in the Coteaux du Languedoc where Viognier is at least officially permitted by the AC regulations. Château Pech Celeyran of La Clape blend it into their Blanc des Cepages de France (£4.85 from Adnams of Southwold). Abbaye de Valmagne (imported by Eldridge Pope of Dorchester) follow an increasingly common practice of blending it with Roussanne. Château de Raissac is experimenting and the Seigneurie de Peyrat have a robust six hectares, enough for several domaines in Condrieu.

Perhaps the most significant thing of all is that these new recruits to the art of growing Viognier have not experienced any of the viticultural disasters reported in Condrieu. Boyer's yield in 1990 was an extremely healthy 50 hectolitres per hectare (having been 32 hl/ha in 1989, the first year of production). He admits that the grapes rot easily and they may have to be sorted carefully before fermentation but finds Viognier much more productive than the normally generous Chardonnay. The more southerly latitude of the Languedoc seems to guarantee much kinder weather while the vine blooms,

But there are several more significant plantations between here and the Viognier's homeland in the northern Rhône. The most famous Vin de Pays property of all, Mas de Daumas Gassac in the hills above Beziers, has been growing Viognier for some time now and it perfumes their extraordinary blended white (£15.10 from Adnams).

One of the first non-Condrieu Viogniers to be sold in Britain was Domaine Ste Anne in Côtes-du-Rhône-Villages country across the river from Orange. Adnams currently list the 1989 at £12.25 while Farr Vintners of London SW1 list the Viognier made at nearby Domaine Ste Estève for around £11.

Much further down the price scale, varietal specialists Delta Domaines (who sell under several labels including Domaine du Bosc and Pierre Besinet) can now offer a 1990 Viognier at around £5 a bottle, as on the current lists of the Wine Society of Stevenage and Tanners of Shrewsbury, but its light, young-vine scent would not satisfy those who lost their hearts to the heady richness of a top Condrieu such as a Vernay or Delas.

The finest non-Condrieu Viognier I have ever tasted came from California where producers such as Joseph Phelps and La Jota have been doing their damnedest with this supposedly fickle vine. The most impressively concentrated (and a wine this smelly needs concentration to stop it being vapid) is Calera's, whose 1989 outshone both Guigal's and Dumazet's 1988 Condrieus in one blind tasting for me. To my knowledge however it has so far been exported only in potentially extremely smelly hand baggage.

October 26, 1991

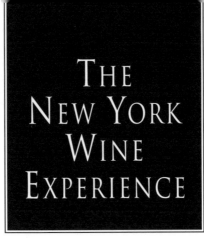

THE NEW YORK WINE EXPERIENCE

Recession? What recession? seemed to be the message from the New York Wine Experience, a long weekend wine jamboree held there last month. In one memorable session lasting little more than an hour, seven wines from the fabulous Domaine de la Romanée Conti, "worth $350,000 retail", were poured into 1000 mouths and rested there for a few seconds before, in many cases, being spat out into polystyrene beakers.

Prices for the thousand tickets for the entire Experience, from Thursday night's tasting via more than 250 wines to Sunday night's gala dinner and wine auction, were set at $750. The waiting list was closed when it reached 2000 people, many of them (ex?) close personal friends of the event's organiser Marvin Shanken, editor and publisher of the American magazine *Wine Spectator*.

The auction, of 67 quite mind-boggling lots (a 'Fantasy Food Tour of France For Two', for example, and a collection of Krug from every vintage since 1928), raised nearly $650,000 for New York's Citymeals-on-Wheels.

And if all of the above sounds excessively quantitative from a pen usually resistant to combining wine and numbers, just remember this was New York. We were usually given the figures before experiencing the quality.

But the quality was more amazing than any number of digits. Each of Bordeaux's first growth proprietors was there, David Orr presenting, with fellow director Hugh Johnson, 324 magnums ("worth $250,000") of Château Latour back to 1961. Each taster was presented with a lump of Latour gravel, a clever 300-kilo idea that must have detonated a few expletives back in Pauillac. Other major sit-down tastings for a thousand encompassed Australia's legend-in-a-bottle Penfolds Grange, an 'outrageous' selection of wines from Italy's most expensive source Gaja and a clutch of top California names.

There were less formal tastings on three successive nights consisting of nearly 200 booths at which one great wine was poured, often by the wine hero who made it, or at least funded the making of it. Louis Latour himself presented his Corton-Charlemagne 1989, while Louis Jadot's version was on tap just round the corner, together with head of the firm André Gagey.

You could take your glass for countless refills of five good vintages of first-growth bordeaux, Bollinger RD 1982 from Christian Bizot, Brunello di Montalcino 1985 from Jacopo Biondi Santi, 1986 Ornellaia or Sassicaia from their respective proprietors - and Christian Moueix was even occasionally spotted at the Dominus table.

Why do they all do it? Presumably because the others do and because times are too hard to run the risks of being left out. If you can persuade one first growth owner you can usually persuade them all in today's spirit of co-operation at the top. That co-operation can cost dear however. Each owner felt impelled to embellish lot 31 - a magnum of the glorious 1945 vintage from each of the first growths - when the bidding showed no signs of rising above the $30,000 cajoled from the room by irrepressible Australian Len Evans for a two-week assault on the liver Down Under. Some of them whiter than others, the first growth owners ended up further committing themselves to flying the successful bidder to Bordeaux to dine at each chateau with "no wine from this century". An expensive way of upholding Gallic pride.

Perhaps the most extraordinary sacrifice on Shanken's altar of excess however was that of the co-owners of the Domaine de la Romanée Conti, Aubert de Villaine and Lalou Bize-Leroy. That they were prepared to open 504 bottles of their wines (only two of which were 'corked'), that sell for several hundreds of pounds a bottle even when babies, is surely a significant comment on the fine wine market. It had taken, we were told, six years to persuade them to expose DRC wines thus (even Khrushchev didn't manage to winkle a bottle out of them when he visited back in the sixties).

The co-owners approached the podium of the ballroom of the Marriott Marquis as though it were the scaffold. Aubert de Villaine began by pointing out, with characteristic courtesy but unmistakeable gloom, that this tasting was "the first, and possibly the last, of its kind. I needn't tell you how strongly our arms had to be twisted." We used up six dozen, for example, of the total production of only 6500 bottles of 1989 RomanéeConti itself, for example, tasting it at a shockingly embryonic stage. And so unwilling, or unable, to release the required six cases of its famous white Montrachet 1983 was 'the Domaine' that these had to rustled up by the American importers.

The logistics of simultaneously serving any eight or nine wines in different glasses at the right temperature and providing the requisite water, tasting sheet, edible blotter and spittoon can be imagined by anyone who has ever tried to serve more than one red and one white at their own dining table. The Domaine added the extra complications of discouraging decanting of their irreplaceable but sedimented bottles. One of America's top sommeliers accordingly proceeded along each row of tasters, pouring reverently from one bottle, followed by a waiter/bearer with the other two assigned to the row.

Beside me as the 1954 Richebourg was poured, a famous French woman chef, now teaching in the Napa Valley, burst into tears at the childhood memories it evoked. On my other side, a big formaggio in one of the major Italian import companies was slipped double measures of 1979 La Tâche by a sommelier keen to impress.

Could such an event take place in Europe? One of Burgundy's great names and I agreed it would be a different animal entirely if ever exposed to British amateurism, Latin timekeeping or France's *tendresse* for speeches. Although if any British wine merchant could pull it off, Lay and Wheeler of Colchester could, to judge from their recent 20-glass Château Palmer tasting and dinner for 170.

November 30, 1991

SIC TRANSIT VINUM

Jean-Paul Amiel is no fool, which is why he is so painfully aware that he was born a generation too late. At 44 he's a *negociant en vin*, a bulk wine merchant of the sort for which the world no longer has a need. He sits in a recently air-conditioned but indicatively quiet office next to the gloomy warehouses that constitute the family business in Trèbes, on one of the busier roads through southern France's vineland.

In each warehouse is a forest of vats three storeys high that are designed for blending, according to a few standard recipes, wine at its most basic, vin de table that can sell for as little as 24 francs (£2.40) per degree/hectolitre(100 litres). A litre of wine containing 10 degrees of alcohol therefore sells for around 24 pence, proportionately more for stronger stuff. A wine's average stay in one of these vats, built by a local workforce that has found new work building swimming pools, is one week before being pumped into a road tanker and trundled off to one of Jean-Paul Amiel's shrinking list of customers.

His father Roger was the lucky one, at the helm in the giddy days of the sixties when the French annually drank an average of more than 120 litres a head of vin de table alone (it is now nearer 50) and the words wine and quality were rarely, if ever, conjoined. Now retired, and an enthusiastic amateur restaurant critic, Roger unkindly tells his son that the negociant profession is a profession for fools, as they hear of the demise of yet another *negociant en vin*. There are only 17 left in the whole of the Aude département now. In the good old days there were 20 in Carcassonne alone and another 30 in nearby Lézignan-Corbières.

Today, and for the forseeable future, it is not wine merchants who are fortunate but wine drinkers. An unprecedented peak in the quality of wine produced has coincided with all manner of forces designed to keep prices down, including the prospect of more and better wine from eastern Europe and South Africa that will doubtless be seeking international favour, and customers.

The casual observer in Britain or America might be tempted to think that the Amiels of this world have fallen victim to competition from the much-publicised winemakers of the New World, but the explanation for the stagnant pond at the bottom end of the wine market is very much closer to Trèbes than that - all around it in fact, in the vineyards of southern France, now in direct competition with Italy, Spain and Greece too, that are quite simply still producing far more table wine than could possibly be consumed by today's increasingly discerning consumers.

Brussels has been grappling worthily with the problem of its most fragmented agricultural sector, dominated not just by peasants but by extremely militant peasants (as witness two bombings, symbolic rather than lethal, in the Midi last summer). There have been subsidies to distil wine surpluses for over a decade and, more recently, financial rewards for grubbing up inferior, overproductive vine types that currently act as a welcome retirement bonus for Europe's less committed vine farmers.

But the wine lake is still there: 28 million hectolitres, or enough to fill 3.7 billion bottles with surplus plonk in the EEC alone last year. And that was more than 10 per cent of the world's entire 1990 vintage, and far more than the total production of America and Australia combined. Theoretically at least, therefore, 23 million were earmarked for distillation at the end of last year, mainly in Spain, France's new viticultural *bête noire*, but also in Italy, France and Greece. But no giant leaps of imagination are needed to conceive of ways in which this physically and geographically cumbersome scheme and its vine-pulling counterpart are open to abuse.

The problem is much more fundamental however. Just as a target is met a new one has to be set, as the world's total wine consumption continues to fall. Every one of the world's six biggest markets for wine - France, Italy, the US, USSR, Spain and Argentina - either shrank dramatically in the eighties or is doing so now. And today in France, the cradle of wine in the modern world, more than half of all adults say they never drink wine, and those who do are much more likely to eke out a bottle marked Appellation Contrôlée from a specified place and producer than to use wine as a past generation did, as an anonymous lubricant bought in quantity by the plastic cubitainer or returnable star-embossed litre.

Total British consumption of wine may be small by comparison (12 litres per head per year) but it is still growing, just, and a far lower proportion of adults than in France, only 32 per cent, say they never drink wine.

But in Britain, as in France, as everywhere, quality is now the key. As poor Amiel Jr knows only too well, vin ordinaire is a ghost stalking only the seedier margins of the wine trade outside France.

The house white of Britain's most lauded off-licence chain Oddbins is not a nameless table wine but a perfectly respectable wine from a single Gascon proprietor (who must still be rubbing his eyes in disbelief at the size of this particular order, and the investments he can make in improved technology as a result). Even the world's biggest producers of wine for the masses, the brothers Gallo, so powerful that they can manufacture not just 'Hearty Burgundy' in the hot Central Valley of California but also the flagons to put it in, are planning an estate-bottled wine priced at $60 a bottle.

Marketing theorists have always had trouble making wine fit their formulae. Just to prove it, branded wines have all but evaporated in a sophisticated market such as Britain, leaving the odd brewers' label to give publicans something they can get to grips with. The Corridas and Rocamars have been replaced by such brand names as Chardonnay (the ubiquitous grape variety, once Burgundy's speciality, now available with almost any regional accent), Sainsbury's (the supermarket chain and still Britain's biggest wine retailer) and Blush (a new name for rose). That the Oxford graduate who was once brand manager for Hirondelle and Mateus Rosé now represents the wines of the late Baron Philippe de Rothschild in Britain is a nice illustration of the sea change in wine's fortunes in the last 15 years - as is the fact that the company originally responsible for Mateus Rose, the success story of the sixties, is now concentrating on developing wines that show what only Portugal can offer.

Paradoxically, now that wine is not actually drunk in the quantities it was in the seventies (and even then total world wine production was lower than the peak of a century before, brought to such a sudden halt by the advent of the vine-chewing phylloxera louse, now apparently making a major comeback), it has never enjoyed such widespread acclaim and respect.

Thanks to the distribution revolution, wine may be available to all, but it sure is smart. Someone who knows about wine is not a drinker but a connoisseur. Wine, intriguingly elevated in this respect above food, has joined art and antiques as a recognised accoutrement of social ascent. Christie's and Sotheby's run courses in it, on it and expensively awash with it.

Although there have been repeated attempts to associate the use of wine with abuse of its most potent component, particularly in the US where even bottles of Château Lafite have to carry warning labels and, curiously, in France where every wine advertisement now has to carry a health warning, there are few signs of tarnish on wine's glossy image.

Connoisseurship has become an international sport. Coteries of wine collectors - notably German, American and Scandinavian - gather in flashy restaurants around the globe for the vinous equivalent of stamp swapping. One of them, Hardy Rodenstock, throws a three day wine tasting party every September at an alpine lodge whose bottle bank this year was filled with nineteenth century magnums of fine bordeaux. Charity auctions provide thousands of American wine lovers with an excuse to dress up and spend absurd but tax-efficient sums on their favoured beverage.

For the first time in wine's history, there is an international forum for discussion of it, and if the participants don't understand each others' language, then they can always communicate by numbers. Wine producers today are only too aware of the public scoreboard on which their efforts are rated. Wine shows, journals and newsletters can make or break the reputation of a wine or wine producer. The publication of each issue of *The Wine Advocate*, a newsletter written by American marathon taster Robert Parker, is immediately followed by a flurry of fax activity around the world as merchants and collectors fight over the frustratingly finite allocations of wines to which he's given more than 90 points out of 100. (Those he scores below 80 on the other hand are practically unsaleable in the US and any stocks remaining there have presumably to be shipped off to nascent, non-anglophone markets - desert islands perhaps.)

In a contracting market in which consumers are becoming ever more sophisticated and informed, it is hardly surprising that wine tastes so good nowadays. But the dramatic rise in wine quality at all levels - even lowly vin de table - would have happened even if wine writing were outlawed (as some consumers, scornful of the wilder, oakier, more blackcurranty shores of winespeak, would like to see it).

From the consumer's point of view, California's wine renaissance, that made wine as important in the state as it had been a century earlier, was the best thing that could have happened to French wine. For a while in the early eighties, particularly when the dollar was weak of course, any reasonably cosmopolitan French wine producer was in a permanent state of panic about what miracle of wine achievement might be on its way across the Atlantic. The French wine industry was already gearing itself up, investing admirably in training and technology, but the sheer noise generated whenever a California Cabernet Sauvignon 'beat' the first growth bordeaux on which it had been modelled hastened the dramatic improvements in modern winemaking that can be tasted in almost every bottle sold today.

The most obvious promulgator of techniques that make even that minority of wines worth keeping also worth drinking young, has been Bordeaux's Professor Emile Peynaud, not just an academic and author but consultant from Château Margaux in the Médoc to Château Carras in Macedonia.

Improvements in the vineyard have been slower to effect (a heat exchanger can be installed within days, vines take three years before they even produce a decent crop and are then expected to earn their keep for 30 years or so) but they too reflect a level of international communication and co-operation that would have been unthinkable even 20 years ago when the average Burgundian proprietor claimed ignorance of his counterparts even in the same village (although some of the older ones still do).

Not only do vine growers, wine producers and technicians communicate openly at events which for once really are symposia, there has also been a marked increase in the last five years in the physical exchange of expertise. Wine producers with serious ambitions, wherever their roots, routinely and unashamedly expose themselves to both New and Old World techniques, the most marked difference between them rapidly becoming the time allowed for lunch. And really ambitious winemakers can in less than 12 months make their mark on two vintages, one in each hemisphere.

This may be part of the reason why Australia's influence on the world's wines seems out of proportion to its annual production of less than two per cent of them. A near obsession with technical probity is spreading slowly but surely from the tasting benches of South Australia around Europe and beyond as more and more Australian-trained winemakers infiltrate cellars smellier than they're used to. And it is to Australia and New Zealand that the West Coast wine industry owes its new-found toy, 'canopy management', a sort of vineyard flower arranging designed to maximise both quality and quantity, regarded with deep suspicion in classical wine regions.

The Millionaire Peasant Syndrome, whereby financially successful and otherwise intelligent individuals choose to write off part of their fortune scratching dirt and producing wine, has been most marked in the United States. The explosion of new wineries in California in the eighties was almost entirely due to romance, the fashionably bucolic aura that surrounds a commodity whose total production and marketing processes can be controlled by one person - as well of course as to helpful tax structures and rising property values (these people aren't idiots).

But the syndrome is clearly a powerful one. Despite the all-too-obvious problems of over-supply, Millionaire Peasant Syndrome has broken out in, of all places, France. The head of Cartier regards his showpiece wine farm in Cahors as his spiritual home. And how has property developer Jacques Ribourel decided to spend his payout from the Groupe de Mèze? On buying and upgrading hundreds of hectares of vines on the Mediterranean coast of course, not far from those of funny film star Pierre Richard, who doubtless discusses the relative merits of various grape presses with Gérard Depardieu, whose own wine château is in the Loire.

During the eighties France's smartest vineyards, mostly in Bordeaux, were raided by the banks, the insurance companies and, to a lesser extent, by foreigners (Suntory's purchase of Château Lagrange did wonders for the quality of this second growth bordeaux, and is already serving Japan's growing connoisseur class).

Vine-growing has become increasingly productive, by means that are considerably less ecologically sound than its image suggests. Stocks are such that even periodic frosts of the severity experienced last spring in eastern France are unlikely to boost the price of wine to levels that will sufficiently justify the investments made by some of these corporate investors in upgrading so many wine properties both practically and cosmetically. (My dear, one simply has to have a halogen-lit cask hall and marble tasting room.)

The fine wine firm Cordier which includes Bordeaux's famous second growth Château Gruaud-Larose but also, typically, an American winery (Texas this time), is openly on the market, having failed to thrill its new owners, the Suez banking group. It will doubtless be followed by much more unbundling as corporations discover that their finance directors remain unmoved by the glamour of wine. But while they remain such a minority, and such a convincing majority clearly agree to wonder "what the vintners buy, one half so precious as the stuff they sell", there should be no shortage of buyers hankering after a property where they can show just how a 100-point wine is made.

Even Jacques Amiel has responded to the hand-crafted, domainebottled wine world of today by buying a 20-hectare wine farm up in the hills of Minervois appellation. Its annual produce would hardly fill two of his blending vats but his modest red and rosé Domaine Lecugne, which proudly carries his own name on the label, clearly gives him inordinate pleasure already - even if he hasn't yet worked out who exactly is going to drink it.

December 14, 1991
(Weekend FT front page)

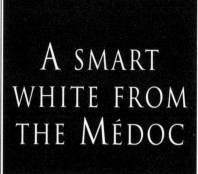

A SMART WHITE FROM THE MÉDOC

Not many people would have the winemaking confidence to launch their new dry white immediately after serving Krug 1955. Come to think of it, not many people nowadays have the financial confidence needed to open even one magnum of Krug, let alone the six or so that preceded the lunchtime launch of Blanc de Lynch Bages. But then its patron, Jean-Michel Cazes, is in an exceptional position.

He is one of the few Bordeaux producers who has been gaining rather than losing control and - possibly thanks to his early working life in the US - is one of a handful who seem part of a world larger than Bordeaux itself. He took over the family properties, notably Château Lynch-Bages, the Pauillac fifth growth widely regarded as a second, back in 1973 when he was in his thirties and has made sure that it has more than kept pace with soaring wine quality since then.

But nowadays much of his time is taken in directing the strikingly ambitious wine interests of the French insurance group AXA, built up by his old classmate Claude Bebear. Across the road from Châteaux Latour and Pichon-Lalande, the Pauillac second growth Château Pichon-Longueville has been rapidly transformed from dangerously derelict to dangerously decadent (the only place where I've climbed a little set of wooden steps into a canopied bath - and was rather surprised not to find a raft of nymphs there offering to scrub my back). The luxurious château building is still surrounded by a sea of mud from which bulldozers and cranes are attempting to create the reality of Cazes' decidedly unMédocain vision of a winery and visitors' centre.

The interior decorators have moved down the road to Margaux's Château Cantenac-Brown, another property that AXA Millésimes is in the process of restoring to its former glory (although this one was cleverly bought just after its vat room had been entirely modernised). As well as Burgundy's Clos de l'Arlot and a clutch of

Bordeaux second wines, AXA controls Châteaux Franc-Mayne in St Emilion, Petit-Village in Pomerol and, scarcely worth mentioning, the 'bourgeois' Pibran in Pauillac, more convenient than most from the point of view of Cazes' own family domain.

That this domain exists at all in Bordeaux's keenly stratified society is something of a miracle. Cazes' great-grandfather was a *montagnol*, an itinerant agricultural worker from one of the poorest parts of the Pyrenees who set up an early sort of Youth Opportunities Programme in Pauillac for the lads back home. His son Jean-Charles did well enough to acquire Lynch-Bages in 1933 (although none of today's glamour attached to the wine business then) and ran it for 40 years. Jean-Michel's father André, still very much a presence at Lynch-Bages, ran the local co-op and was Pauillac's insurance broker.

The evening after his new white's debut, Jean-Michel Cazes was particularly relaxed. Playing with a glass of Roederer Cristal this time, he gazed into one of three scented wood fires that had been lit to give the white shell of Château Cantenac-Brown that lived-in feeling and reflected, "I remember my great-grandfather. He wore sheepskin and hardly spoke French. The Médoc has always been colonised by outsiders; it has no history of its own."

But hang on a minute. The wines of the Médoc are supposed to be red, aren't they? Well only up to a point. Some white grapes have always been grown in among the more famous red ones, or more accurately ink-blue ones, of Bordeaux's northern outcrop of the most famous names in the wine world.

Historically they were either blended in with the red and their existence barely recognised or, like those inherited at Lynch Bages, they were made into white wine for the personal consumption of those who grew them. More recently however the odd white wine has been sent forth into the world to make a statement.

Those of Château Loudenne (GrandMet's isolated wine investment in the outer reaches of the Medoc) and Château Talbot (called Caillou Blanc) are designed to demonstrate the white wine making expertise of the international companies that own them. When the Mentzelopoulos family took over Château Margaux in the late 1970s they deliberately relaunched the domain's white rarity Pavillon Blanc as an early signal of their honourable intentions for this world-famous red wine property.

Blanc de Lynch Bages is simply the latest salvo from the man who has the most impressive range of artillery in Bordeaux. His increasingly hardworked adjutant is winemaker Daniel Llose. Like Cazes, he has roots in Roussillon, having been brought up in Banyuls.

He's made some great red wines, apparently the princess who kissed the once frog-like wines of Pichon-Longueville and Cantenac-Brown. At Lynch-Bages the 1989, 1985, 1988 and 1986 were all stunning in a blind vertical tasting for which the Krug 1955 was the reward.

But, having once done a *stage* in white wine country near Bergerac, Llose was keen to show what he could do with white grapes. Eleven acres of vineyard that didn't qualify for the Pauillac appellation were accordingly planted in 1987 with equal portions Sauvignon, Semillon ("because it ages well") and almost 20 per cent of the traditional Bordelais white Muscadelle. The result is 1800 cases of 1990 Blanc de Lynch Bages, a perfectly competent oak-fermented white that reflects current fashion and the men behind it considerably more than its Médoc roots. A useful, if expensive, first course wine for a Médoc dinner.

January 18, 1992

Blanc de Lynch Bages was soon followed by an almost aggressively oaky, and even more expensive, white from Pauillac, Aile d'Argent from first growth Ch Mouton-Rothschild.

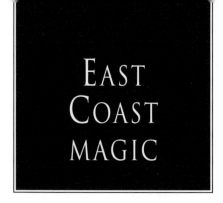

EAST
COAST
MAGIC

New York City stretches into the Atlantic along the Forks of Long Island, effectively the extremes of Manhattan. Here you can find a deli called the Barefoot Contessa selling cooked brussels sprouts and five blends of coffee 'to go', four of them decaffeinated. In cafes roundabout you can order an all-white omelette or cholesterol-free French fries.

Long Island now has a wine industry which, in its way, is also extreme. It is, for a start, extremely young. Wine labels may boast that the relevant vines were planted way back in 1980. (Long Island's first vinifera vineyard for more than a century was planted by Alex and Louisa Hargrave in 1973 who had to wait six years for the next grape grower to come along and prove their sanity.)

It is also, like many a fine wine region, at a climatological extreme. Further north in New York State, winters are too hard for vinifera vines. Only the moderating influence of the surrounding ocean allows the vine species responsible for all the great wines of the world to be grown this far north. Almost all of the vines planted around the Lakes in upstate New York belong to coarser, hardier vine species.

Vines are now encroaching on Long Island's traditionally dominant crop, potatoes - oddly prosaic for a region famous for providing the famous with somewhere, the Hamptons, to spend their weekends with the equally famous.

Today there are well over 1200 acres of vineyard planted, mainly on the North Fork, by about 45 growers and vinified at 15 different wineries. As in so many other areas of commercial endeavour, the early eighties were the boom time. An acre of land was then just $2000 but is today closer to $20,000. The odd Manhattanite, associating the South Fork of Long Island with luxury vacations and wine with the ultimate good time, invested in what turned out to be a dream.

They have now been shaken out, according to Dan Kleck who has worked as a Long Island winemaker since 1979 and is now introducing malolactic fermentation at Palmer winery. "They've sold to more committed people who spend two or three days a week out here and might even drive a tractor once in a while. It's a lot better. Fewer egos."

Now that undesirable outsiders have been seen off, Long Island wine producers are concentrating on the remaining major pests: birds (they're on the main migration route and have to spend about $1000 an acre on special netting); hurricanes (they're meant to happen every 40 years, not every other year); and California.

Any California-trained winemaker comes a terrible cropper in this cool, late-budding climate. "You have to unlearn that California thing," says Kleck. "Our reds need much longer maceration. Our fruit acids are much higher and our alcohols lower." (A Long Island wine more than 12 per cent alcohol is rare indeed, and chaptalisation, adding sugar to raise the final alcohol level, can be the norm some vintages.)

All of this sounds very European and Long Islanders have been keen to stretch welcoming hands over the Atlantic, inviting Bordeaux's top brass to a couple of instructive wine-ins over the last few years, along with Australian viticulturalist Richard Smart who has shown how to use every ray of sunlight to maximise ripening.

The wines taste French in structure, if New World in technology: never heavyweight with crisp, bordering on lean fruit flavours. At the recent New York Wine Experience, a weekend's wine extravaganza organised by The Wine Spectator magazine, 1000 experienced tasters were asked to identify the 1989 Chardonnay from Long Island's exciting new Gristina winery. Well under two per cent guessed it came from Long Island; I thought it was a well-made Chassagne-Montrachet.

Chardonnay seems to be particularly successful here but, unusually, there is potential for dry Gewurztraminers with none of the oily bitterness that dogs California examples. Among red grape varieties, like Washington State 3000 miles west, Merlot has shown most form so far, although Cabernet Franc has its devotees among those not wedded to the clout of California wine. Cabernet Sauvignon can be difficult to ripen fully except in a few very well chosen sites but Long Islanders claim that part of the problem lies in the American consumer's California-shaped perception of how Cabernet Sauvignon should taste. Blending different varieties is a novel sport that will surely become more popular.

Most of the wines retail in the $12-15 bracket, putting them on a par with California's mid-priced varietals but, like their counterparts who make English wine, Long Island wine producers sometimes have to labour against local prejudice. Bridgehampton Winery, one of only two on the South Fork, deliberately sets its cap at the major urban market 70 miles west with the least bucolic image possible, that of Manhattan by night, on several labels. The typically spare but Vivaldi-haunted winery building overlooks the sad remains of a vineyard too prone to frost. Undaunted, the jingle-merchant who owns Bridgehampton has acquired land elsewhere.

It was there that I was told that Bridgehampton reds would be lightening in style. "Our winemaker had a child recently so his search for immortality no longer has to be diverted into his wines."

Most impressive of a wide range of current releases (sic) tasted on Long Island recently were Lenz Gewurztraminer 1989, 1989 Chardonnays from Gristina and Bidwell as well as Gristina's 1988 Cabernet Sauvignon (made at Bridgehampton before their understatedly elegant winery was built), Bridgehampton's light 1989 Merlot, Bedell Cellar's confident and plump 1988 Merlot Reserve and unfinished samples of Palmer 1990 Merlot and 1991 Gewurztraminer. And rainy 1989 has been Long Island's only real problem vintage since 1987.

As far as the vine is concerned, this is clearly a viable if slightly homespun new colony.

January 22, 1992

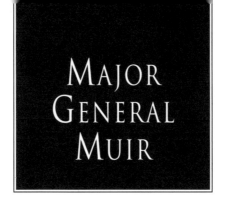

MAJOR GENERAL MUIR

British wine merchant arrived to buy wine at a large French winery. The staff lolled around smoking. The welcome was offhand. The merchant was underwhelmed. Until he mentioned who had sent him. Gitanes were hurriedly stubbed out, the workers set to it like the busiest of bees and a superior echelon of eager management appeared as if by magic. The name capable of galvanising entire workforces in the very unBritish world of wine production is Angela Muir.

Madame Muir (not the easiest surname for a French tongue) is a 43 year old Master of Wine with a very unusual interest, cheap wine. "What really fascinates me", she says, dark eyebrows knit passionately under her Valkyrie mane, "is large volumes of low cost wine that people get physical pleasure from - and that doesn't happen often enough". Uniquely, she has built up a reputation for telling wine producers in the hugely important bottom third of the wine price pyramid, in no uncertain terms, how to make wines that (British) people will actually want to drink. "I start at the critic's end rather than the creator's," is how she explains her particular expertise. "If you happen to have great land, then employing a genius to make great wine is just a question of money. What I'm interested in is working back towards what the consumer wants rather than what the soil will give and how best to express it."

Happily for her the British market is so important, and indicative, to the world's potential wine exporters that, in the first three weeks of last month, she had been to Argentina to help one of the biggest companies there fashion wines for foreign palates with less than ideal equipment (answer: bottle in France); to Chile to find a new source for a British company which may then ask her to source its entire New World range ("very exciting, in an area of the market I really like"); to Czechoslovakia to oversee one of her most innovative schemes to date; to France on a confidential assignment (it's a very competitive market); and finally, and apparently most thrillingly, to an Italian manufacturer of bottling equipment. Angela's eyes light up when describing this visit. "They're very, very good, particularly on computer coordination of bottling lines. We went and had a very interesting look round their machine shops near Verona on the way back from Czechoslovakia."

The Czech project is the first one in which Cellarworld, the company she formed in 1988 with her ex-management accountant husband Peter, has taken a direct stake. It all started during her previous 10-year stint buying wine ("proactively, like the Oddbins boys") for Allied-Lyons where she was most famous for dragging a huge Spanish bodega into the late twentieth century by promising to buy the resulting crisp 1982 white revamp for the Don Cortez label. (Her unrivalled buying power at Grants of St James's Ltd was of course why producers initially listened to her instinctively didactic comments on their wines.)

The road to Czechoslovakia went via Ethiopia. Someone ("it's always silly - a friend of a friend, or someone wanting a reciprocal deal") asked Angela to evaluate some Ethiopian wines. The wines stayed in Ethiopia but 18 months ago she was asked by a related contact to look at a range of wines from a Czechoslovakia desperate for trade with the west. "Despite the ghastly labels, and some unpleasant winemaking aromas of sorbates etcetera, I realised there was some very good intense fruit there. I said I'd write them a report if they'd pay for me to go and spend four days there. You can learn a lot in four days if you really decide to get to grips with it."

Yes, ma'am. Or rather, yes, Major General, to which rank Angela has been elevated by her obedient if slightly stunned colleagues at the Slovakian wineries from which she has coaxed four remarkably clean, fresh westernised varietals that are just hitting the shelves of better Victoria Wine shops at under £3 a bottle. If the first three days' sales are indicative, she may turn out to be the saviour of the Czech wine industry (about half the size of the long-westernised Bulgarian one).

The Muir Czech revolution encompassed such refinements as an awesome respect for hygiene, a proper understanding of filtration, sterile bottling and under-utilised equipment and whirlwind labelling applications to Brussels. The bottling lines have already, miraculously, been upgraded to meet the most demanding British supermarket delegation. She also had to make changes in the tasting and dining rooms. "I told them we needed proper big tasting glasses, not thimbles. Also that we needed something to spit into - and that we certainly didn't need cat stew."

The Muirs live, with their cats, in deepest Surrey. Peter Muir is clearly vital to the business and, like many palates exposed to wine through their partners', an impressive blind taster. His formidable wife views the fine wine market as a "minor interest" and the wine she chooses to drink is, typically, fizzy and copious.

If she is right about the future of the wine market there will be a need for more and more consumer-driven consultants of her ilk. "Wine will be used more and more as a luxury and it's going to be one hell of a struggle for survival by vineyard owners. The market will increasingly demand reasonable prices and that wine tastes nice. There is lots of trauma ahead for producers who can't make that adjustment."

Cellarworld operates from the same address as the useful wine shop and wine school at Fulham Road Wine Centre, 899/900 Fulham Road, London SW6 Tel. 0171-384 2588.

March 7, 1992

Angela and Peter Muir found it impossible to continue as retailers and now concentrate on consultancy.

THROUGH
A GLASS
UNWILLINGLY

I f I could have one luxury it would be infinite quantities of the finest, most delicate, most perfectly shaped wine glasses in the world, plus the all-important space in which to store them. The Tyrolean glassblowers who would therefore have to get blowing are those responsible for the Riedel Sommelier range, an everexpanding set of shapes individually designed by Austrian Georg Riedel as 'tasting tools' to maximise the pleasure given by specific styles of wine.

Fortunately, unlike the Burgundian 'Impitoyables' range which really is merciless in its assault on the sensitive eye as well as in exposing any wine fault, Riedel's glasses satisfy aesthetic criteria too - although he claims this is a secondary consideration. His burgundy glass is on permanent show at New York's Museum of Modern Art.

As luxuries go, Riedel's pingingly delicate and efficacious handblown Sommelier glasses are not that expensive. Peter Jones, the London SW3 householder's mecca, sells the glasses specially designed to enhance young red bordeaux at £24.50 each, as opposed to their (excellent value) equivalents with a machine-made stem from the Vinum range at £11.50.

There is fierce competition in glassware, or 'stemware' as it is known in America, at the top end of the market. What makes Georg Riedel so attractive in my eyes is only partly his glasses, and nothing whatever to do with his obviously talented tailor. It is his conviction that wine glasses, even the finest, most delicate and most expensive, are best washed not by hand but in a dishwasher.

According to the books, and the concensus of traditional wine lore, dishwasher and even detergent are dirty words. The only way to treat a used wine glass properly, they say, is to wash it throughly, rinse it in very hot water and then to polish it dry with a perfectly clean, detergent-free linen teatowel. (In fact wine traditionalists have probably saved the Irish linen business from extinction.) I have therefore spent years feeling extremely guilty about my lazy habit of stuffing as many wine glasses as possible into a machine rather than dedicating long mornings-after to an orgy of rinsing and polishing. It came as the most blessed relief to me then, akin to a sudden papal edict licensing sex before marriage, to hear Georg Riedel's revelation, made among the power lunchers at New York's Four Seasons restaurant after a trial of his Pinot Noir glass conducted by such international wine stars as Robert Drouhin, Len Evans, Angelo Gaja, the head of Louis Jadot, Tim Mondavi and Christian Moueix. (This man knows the wine world.)

He gave as evidence of his devotion to mechanical lavage, the fact that he'd just lent 3000 glasses to a wine weekend in an alpine hotel and had them shipped back, still reeking of firstgrowth claret, to the firm's glass washing machines. He did admit that the domestic dishwasher at Schloss Riedel is often too small for his needs but says that so long as we fill surplus dirty glasses with water overnight, they can safely be put through the dishwasher in the morning. Conversely, it is the humidity that harms the glass after washing, so glasses should ideally be unloaded as soon as possible after each cycle.

Riedel's leaflets even spell out which dishwasher models will accommodate racks specially designed for glasses such as his and such is his devotion to detail that he specifies the order numbers of the parts. Miele G530-567 and G579-590 are wine-glass friendly according to Riedel's copious literature, as are all Bosch and Siemens dishwashers.

My Hotpoint (a phrase I somehow never thought I'd find myself using) leaves even my finest glasses whole, sparkling and free of the inimical smell of detergent - although admittedly it is supplied via a water softener. The secret is to use detergent sparingly (and of course to make sure that the rest of the stuff in the dishwasher isn't covered with coffee grains or leftover food). Our champagne glasses, too tall for the machine, always look horribly besmirched after their hand wash by comparison.

Another firm that takes the (all too rare) wine lover's view of top quality glassware is John Jenkins of Rogate near Petersfield in Hampshire. John Jenkins' Bohemian Classic range, at about the same price as Riedel's Vinum, is useful for its good-value handmade all-rounders. The Jenkins team refuse to go on the record endorsing dishwashers, but they do use them.

They of all people will know that thinner, in a glass context, does not mean more fragile; Riedel and Baccarat glasses will often bounce if dropped, which is by no means the case with the Esso giveaways.

Riedel's Sommelier and Vinum glasses, John Jenkins' Bohemian Classic glasses, are stocked by Peter Jones of London SW3, Harrods and a host of good wine merchants.

March 14, 1992

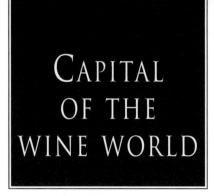

CAPITAL
OF THE
WINE WORLD

On Tuesday Henri Jayer, the most famous winemaker in Burgundy, will be celebrating his seventieth birthday at a smart French restaurant. Nothing remarkable in that perhaps, except that the restaurant he has chosen is not in Saulieu, Chagny or even Paris. It is Le Gavroche in London. Last Monday the most influential man in the Médoc, Jean-Michel Cazes, trekked across the Channel to convince Sotheby's customers of the worth of his wines. On Thursday it was the turn of Christian de Billy of Champagne Pol Roger, while two of Germany's best-rated wine producers, Ernst Loosen and Gunderloch's Fritz Hasselbach, have been buzzing around London all week.

To the busier bees of the wine world, London is the honey pot. Only Germany imports more wine in total than the United Kingdom (950 million litres of wine 1990 to our 640 million) but most of it is pretty basic stuff. And Britain, as well as being the prime market for good quality bordeaux, burgundy, Loire, sherry, port and antipodean wines, has just one obvious centre of connoisseurship, London.

Words have to be chosen carefully here since London cannot claim a monopoly on Britain's top quality wine merchants. East Anglia and Edinburgh have more than their fair share of first-rate vintners, but the great majority of wine activity takes place in the capital.

This sort of slurping and spitting is at its most obvious at the tastings, lunches and dinners that the wine world takes so much for granted. The London Wine Trade Diary is crammed with these godsends for the thirsty, sometimes as many as seven a day in the high seasons of early summer and autumn (although in August it is blank). The Diary, aimed at preventing the most frustrating clashes, is kept by the Wine Promotion Board in offices next door to Vintners' Hall in Vintry Ward, the medieval wine quarter of the City of London. Only wool was traded more than wine when the king of England was also king of Aquitaine.

The wine trade moved gradually east and west of Southwark Bridge. And nowadays the international conglomerates soused in wine have decamped from London altogether to bottling plants and bonded warehouses in places such as Worksop and Southampton. But subterranean London is still shaped by its wine trade history.

A few feet below the pavement, much of St James's is or was a wine cellar. The Stafford Hotel in St James's Place has particularly atmospheric cellars, still in working use, which can be hired for anything from a serious wine tasting to a teetotal reception. Ultra-traditional wine merchants Justerini & Brooks and Berry Bros & Rudd, both still employing cellar staff, face each other across St James's Street, their landmark premises signalling very obviously which was founded in 1749 and which 'in the XVII Century'. Berry Bros in particular, with its bare boards, mostly bare shelves, ledgers and Beau Brummel's weight records is worth a place on the least bibulous tourist's London itinerary.

On particularly busy days in the Wine Trade Diary a network of inter-tasting tunnels would be useful, for there are more cellars, in varying stages of their working life, around Trafalgar Square, the City and, typically, in dank railway arches, notably around Tooley Street just south of London Bridge. One of these rattling, tenebrous warehouses, Trapps, houses the 'cellars' of thousands of wine collectors, some as far afield as Hong Kong and San Francisco, as well as the constantly changing stocks of the auction houses Christie's and Sotheby's which have been crucial in maintaining London's supremacy in the wine world.

Christie's have fine wine sales in the City and, mainly, in King Street, St James's. Sotheby's main sales are at New Bond Street, W1. James Christie's very first sale in 1766 included 'a large Quantity of Madeira and high Flavour'd Claret' and the dominant wine auctioneer would by now have 225 years of continuous wine sales under its gavel were it not for restrictions on auctions after the second world war.

Today, if first growth Bordeaux chateau owners want to send a ripple of their claret round the world of wine, they are most likely to begin it in London, either by organising a high-profile auction of some particularly rare older vintages, or with a tasting or dinner.

The sadness for many of us is that we are too busy justifying our place on the invitation list to take full advantage of every glass available. My dream is a retirement not so complete that the invitations stop.

March 28, 1992

MONTRACHET'S COSMIC COMPOST

For the organic wine movement Anne-Claude Leflaive must be the best thing to have happened so far. Or perhaps the second best thing after this year's saga of fungicide traces in various Italian wines. Organic, ecologically-conscious vine cultivation has been increasing in recent years, but mainly on the fringes of the wine world. Anne-Claude Leflaive, new co-manager of the world-famous Domaine Leflaive in Puligny-Montrachet, is so far the only major wine producer in Bordeaux or Burgundy publicly to embrace what to many seem self-evident principles of planet protection. And her new system for Leflaive's enviable spread of top quality vineyards is not just any old organic one, but the Steiner-inspired *biodynamie* which integrates wholly natural treatments with the movements of the cosmos.

A warm, frank woman of 36, she is the eldest child of the courtly Vincent who ran the Domaine Leflaive until serious illness in 1989 took him away from the day-to-day decisions he by then shared with his nephew Olivier (who also runs the separate wine merchant business Olivier Leflaive Frères).

Burgundian inheritance laws are famously complicated; Anne-Claude gives the impression that the US presidential race is relatively clean-cut compared to the question of Vincent's succession. But in June 1990 she finally managed to convince her family as well as herself that this was the job she had been seeking all her life. Now she has managed to solve one of the potential problems (by living near Nuits-St-Georges rather than Dijon where her engineer husband works) even if she has substituted another (her third child is expected in August).

She had for years 'done the vintage' at the Domaine, and even spent the freezing winter of 1989 in the vineyards there immersing herself literally in the all-important soil, as well as forging links with the vineyard staff that were to stand her in good stead when she came to apply her new methods. "I think I am very tied to this village", she admits with proud resignation. Even when she took a sabbatical sailing trip round the Caribbean with her husband and children, she claims, "all the time I was thinking of the vines".

Her rapport with the Domaine's dedicated and reserved winemaker Pierre Morey and with Olivier mean that she can dedicate a high proportion of her four days a week to those vineyards - to which has just been added the final piece in Leflaive's jigsaw puzzle of grands crus, an extremely expensive pocket handerchief of the most famous white burgundy vineyard of all, about a fifth of an acre, or £600,000 worth, of fully mature vines in Le Montrachet itself.

"If only Leflaive had some Montrachet" has long been a refrain of the world's wine enthusiasts, eager to see the Domaine's imcomparably elegant style of winemaking applied to the greatest vineyard of all. There won't be much to show - hardly 30 cases of 1991, picked by Anne-Claude and Pierre Morey themselves one memorable sunny afternoon last October - but even in a recession they can presumably expect some help with the interest payments when the wine is finally offered for sale or, more likely, allocated at around £200 a bottle.

A further acquisition of six mature *ouvrées* of Folatières has more than doubled the Leflaive holdings in this Puligny-Montrachet premier cru vineyard since Anne-Claude took over from her father.

I asked how Vincent, who still occupies his vast desk in the Domaine's handsome first floor office, had reacted to his daughter's conversion to cow dung, camomile, nettles and the lunar cycle and was surprised to hear "He is a hundred times more convinced than I am. I always have a image of my father sitting outside after dinner looking up at the stars. I think he understands their language."

For Anne-Claude the revelation came at a lecture given by the appropriately named Claude Bourguignon, warning that the soil of Burgundy had become so worn out by over-application of fertilisers, pesticides and fungicides that it was effectively nearly dead. Since then she has organised a conference for fellow Burgundian producers, as well as a pilgrimage to see organic vineyards such as Huet's in Vouvray. She believes it was the rugged rationality of ex-maths teacher Noel Pinguet of Huet that convinced so many of her neighbours that the principles were sound. They are yet to put them into practice but some, such as Christophe Roumier of Domaine Georges Roumier and Pascal Marchand at Clos des Epeneaux are moving in that direction.

Certainly, there is many a Burgundian peasant who still bottles his wine according the moon and the wind, so the region should be more biodynamically receptive than, say, Bordeaux where fewer decision-makers actually get their hands dirty.

It is far too early to be sure of the results of the Leflaive experiment on a selected two and a half acres, although Anne-Claude notes that the all-important yield is reduced, the vine leaves and soil already look quite different and she thinks she can detect more direct flavours in the fruit. Some Leflaive fans may worry than the famous elegance could be compromised by this new regime but Simon Loftus points out in his fascinating new book 'Puligny-Montrachet' (£19.99 Ebury Press) that evolution is inevitable and that we should rejoice in the 'one essential continuum in the history of Domaine Leflaive, the passion for quality'.

Anne-Claude's medium-term ambition is certainly appropriate to a continuum - to establish what is literally a co-operative compost heap in Puligny - and she describes it with real animation. "Like in the Middle Ages when they recycled everything. It was fantastic in the Middle Ages, you know, even for women. I think I should have lived in the Middle Ages."

Leflaive's white burgundies can be bought, at £20 and up a bottle, from merchants such as Adnams of Southwold, John Armit of London W11, Corney & Barrow of EC1 and Lay & Wheeler of Colchester.

May 9, 1992

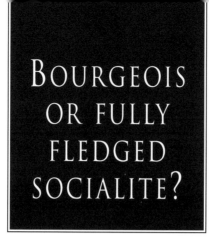

BOURGEOIS OR FULLY FLEDGED SOCIALITE?

My Bordeaux broker friend hadn't even heard of Château Lilian-Ladouys. "Oh no, not another cru bourgeois having money lavished on it," he said gloomily, referring to Bordeaux's underclass of more than 200 châteaux officially ranked a notch below the 60-odd châteaux, or crus, classified in 1855. "All they ever do is prove there really is a difference between even the best crus bourgeois and the crus classés."

Perhaps he was thinking of Château Clarke, a cru bourgeois in Listrac into which Swiss banker Baron Edmond de Rothschild has immersed his not inconsiderable personal income from the family's famous crus classé Château Lafite-Rothschild only to prove, some would say, that in terms of wine quality if not geography, the Listrac hinterland is very much more than 15 kilometres away from the peak of Pauillac.

The man who has decided to sink what he made out of electronic payment systems into an unglorious patch of St Estèphe presumably has other crus bourgeois in mind. Châteaux Monbrison, Sociando-Mallet, Haut-Marbuzet, Chasse-Spleen and of course Gloria can command, purely on the basis of the quality of wine produced, higher prices than the most lacklustre (although admittedly underperforming) crus classés.

Until 1990 Christian Thiéblot was based in Paris and chairman of Sodinforg, a computer company with a turnover of £85 million that is now part of Paribas. He and his Swiss wife Lilian had already tried for two years to make a go of a wine property in the Bas Médoc, the boondocks of Bordeaux, but realised that to have any chance of making both an impact and fine wine, they'd have to invest in one of the Haut-Médoc's four famous communes Margaux, St Julien, Pauillac or St Estèphe.

The chance to acquire 10 hectares (25 acres) of vineyard entitled to the appellation St Estèphe seemed too good to pass up and they decided to buy Château Ladouys in May 1989 without even seeing inside the rather handsome eighteenth century building. Because the property had belonged to the head of St Estèphe's relatively important co-op, where the Ladouys grapes were vinified, the property was effectively without winemaking equipment. "There wasn't even a screwdriver here - nothing!" say the Thiéblots.

But the co-op connection brought an unexpected bonus. The newcomers let it be known around the village that they would be happy to buy more vineyard. And since the Marquis de St Estèphe co-op had so many elderly 'adherents' willing to swap hard weekend work for a tidy little nest egg, the Thiéblots were overwhelmed by vendors. They now own about 50 hectares (125 acres) of mature vineyard, dotted about the commune, which makes Château Lilian-Ladouys one of St Estèphe's biggest properties. (Christian decided to add his wife's first name to the original name - perhaps more graceful than Château Ladouys-Thiéblot which would have been the result of the more usual practice.)

To the villagers of St Estèphe Christian Thiéblot must seem like a fairy godfather. It must be odd to live surrounded by new cars, house extensions and small businesses that you have personally financed.

The unexpected success of the Ladouys expansion plan has meant that architect's drawings have had to be dramatically revised. In the first summer they had just two months to erect a working winery and were rewarded with the miraculously ripe and successful 1989 vintage. They now however have not just one vatroom but two, with more stainless steel than most crus classés and enough tasteful tiling to line every kitchen-diner in north London. In the uplit cask hall the barrels are scrubbed and stained with perfectionism reminiscent of Mouton. In the bottle store, the visitor is urged to take note of the quality of the bottles, the thickness of the purple paper in which they are wrapped, the quality of the wooden cases and the diversity of bottle sizes available.

What started as a mild pipedream has become a major gamble. Christian Thiéblot is staking FF110 million, and calmly says he expects to start making money ("about six per cent ROI") in 1994.

They have already shown they can make good wine. With Sylvie Franchini as oenologist and other local technical expertise, they have produced a 1989 and 1990 that taste as though no expense were spared in the making of them: enormously ripe, spicy monsters with the tannins needed for a long life mainly smothered by the fruit. They are certainly wines to change the minds of those who dismiss St Estèphe as hard and acid in youth, and have already been written up in both American and French wine magazines. The 1989 was recently voted top of a comparative tasting of 1989 crus bourgeois by the magazine *Decanter*.

But in a market awash with competently made claret from the two glorious 1989 and 1990 vintages, who will soak up the wine from this as yet unknown cru bourgeois? This consideration may be behind the Thiéblots' avowed intent not to plunge into the general marketplace of Bordeaux merchants but to try to seek out specific importers instead. "We want first of all to sell to the British and the Belgians because they are the connoisseurs," says Thiéblot. "The French just say we're too expensive."

I wonder whether a) he realises that the FT is printed in France and b) the French haven't got a point. The Thiéblots' pricing policy is, to say the least, ambitious. If I understood it aright, they decided that to avoid disenchanting one sector of the market by putting up their prices once they'd established themselves, they'd put their price up before establishing themselves. Accordingly, the opening price of the first, 1989 vintage was 57 francs, the same, presumably intentionally, as the much more established cru bourgeois Château Sociando-Mallet which makes it about £12 a bottle from British merchants such as Winecellars of London SW18 (0181-871 2668) and Summerlee Wines of Earls Barton (01604 810488).

Aesthetics, posh tasting room, bilingual polychrome illustrated booklet, second label (Château Naudet), lunches at Taillevent for France's top wine writers - Christian Thiéblot's got the lot. Now all he needs is his ROI.

Importers are Freddy Price of London W5 0181 997 7889; Mampaey of Belgium 02.466.58.58; Zeter of Germany 6321.885.58; Cave SA 022.64.00.66 of Gland and Testuz SA 21.799.20.21 of Cully in Switzerland; Reserve and Selection of Montreal, Canada 514.3993.

May 18, 1992

THE GENTLE GIANT OF PARK AVENUE

T he US may no longer enjoy its mid-eighties status as the wine world's biggest spender, but Abdallah H Simon is still the lynchpin of the international wine trade. This is not just because he is such an important customer - his Château & Estate Wines Company sells up to 40 per cent of America's imports of fine wine, notably classed-growth bordeaux - but also because he is the only wine merchant to be taking decisions crucial to the world's wine trade with the benefit of four decades' experience.

A measure of the breadth of that experience, and its importance, is that Simon must be the only Chevalier of France's elite Legion d'Honneur to be a graduate of England's Southport College, the University of Beirut, the Iraqi army and, when he finally managed to escape rising anti-semitism in his native Bagdad in 1943, the US forces in Europe.

It was a seminal bottle of Ch Latour 1929 that propelled him from the family textile business into the fledgling US wine trade to which he has applied his business skills for 40 years, 18 of them creating Château & Estate, an empire to his own specifications within America's leviathan of liquor, Seagram.

Revered by all who matter in America's wine business, he is of course courted assiduously by some of the world's grandest wine producers. It would be reasonable therefore to expect a certain brash arrogance in the man, but from Bordeaux to the Bronx it is agreed that the softly-spoken 70 year-old Ab Simon is, above all else, a gentleman.

The US wine trade needs Simon. His honour and old world manners legitimise it. His warehouses feed it. His salesmen service it. His company effectively finances its investment in the now all-important wine futures market. (In many states, including New York, customers cannot be invoiced until the goods are delivered, which may be two years after wine futures are reserved - hence some cancellations, notably of the somewhat stolid 1988s, which have not smoothed Monsieur Simon's biannual path to Bordeaux.)

But the wine world needs the man himself at least as much as the corporation's ability to finance two to four years' stock. His contacts in France are personal and unparalleled. Only a handshake seals C&E's agreements with the 200-plus regular imports listed somewhat incongruously in Seagram's corporate 'Brand Index', from St-Emilion first-growth Ch Ausone to Trimbach's obscure Liqueur de Framboise raspberry syrup.

Jean-Eugène Borie of second-growth Ch Ducru Beaucaillou, for example, one of Bordeaux's more celebrated gentlemen, cannot remember a time when Ab Simon was not his own powerful family's most important customer, nowadays bypassing the traditional Bordeaux merchants by buying through his very own Bordeaux negociant, Vignobles Internationaux.

In New York Ab Simon has additional duties as arbiter, father confessor and sounding board. "Don't ask me about him, I tend to get emotional," says Marvin Shanken, hard-bitten publisher of the industry's most-read publications, "I really love the guy. Whenever I've had controversy as a journalist, whether he represents the wines himself or not, he's always given me an honest appraisal."

And Michael Aaron, head of New York's most traditional smart wine merchant Sherry Lehmann, readily admits "if I formulate an idea about something, I call Ab to see what he thinks. He's a positive asset to the whole industry because he really understands the whole picture."

Understanding the whole picture nowadays means much more than being able to speak French and German and eat with a knife as well as a fork. It means coming to grips with America's increasingly faddish wine buyers, all of whom depend on the same two or three authorities to tell them, through controversial scores out of 100, exactly what to buy. "Scores? Well, look," says Ab Simon with an elegantly magisterial finger. "We're novices in the wine market. Our consumers need to be guided. And the scoring system has definitely been very good for business. We sold out of Haut-Brion 1989 in three days after Robert Parker [the one-man newsletter] gave it a 100."

American collectors today will buy only those years sanctioned by the oracles, which means that C&E sold 1.5 million bottles of 1989 classed growth bordeaux, but less than a fifth of that so far of the less-publicised 1990s. If Ab Simon earned the respect of the wine world by well-publicised efforts to hold down prices of the 1986s, his most expensive mistake was buying the overpriced, unloved 1984s in order to keep his allocations with the châteaux. That small but vigorous American minority prepared to pay $20 for a bottle of bordeaux nowadays has been primed to scorn 1984, which is why C&E's 1984s (even the fabulous Château Pétrus of which C&E are given 90 per cent of the US allocation) are still being offloaded, via French and even British merchants, into French supermarkets.

Ab Simon has learnt his lesson. "The 1984s highlighted for us that the US consumer needs a strong, clear image of a vintage. For that reason we won't be buying the 1991s, except for taking up our small allocations of the first growths, because the image of the 1991 harvest is so confused. And the 1991s are coming out at prices that are too high, higher than the 1987s which are not exactly selling, as we say, like hot cakes. The 1991 vintage is not for us in terms of futures and I don't think it is for the US market even after it has been bottled." (Take that, Bordeaux.)

He was to communicate all this to Christian Moueix of Ch Pétrus over lunch the next day (he lunches about twice a week at the famous Four Seasons restaurant just below his quiet Park Avenue office). That night he and his deservedly popular wife Francine, with whom he has always insists on travelling, were still hosting a 15-wine dinner for 50 at 11.30. Those of us three decades younger found it quite punishing.

But Ab Simon says he has no plans to retire, and that last year's heart surgery should have set him up for many years more. "I try very hard to do the right thing" he claims as his motto. But there are those in the wine trade who feel that no eventual successor could possibly match his probity - and there are those who fear an option with very much more serious consequences, that Ab Simon alone is capable of keeping Seagram's faith in the exceptionally labour- and capital-intensive fine wine market.

May 23, 1992

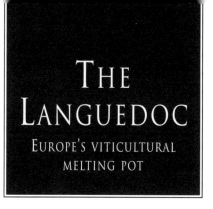

THE LANGUEDOC

EUROPE'S VITICULTURAL MELTING POT

I'm hurtling round a roundabout on the outskirts of Narbonne one morning in James Herrick's Alfa Romeo when his car phone bleeps. "Allo? G'day, mate, what are you doing up so late? (Pause) What are the Baumés at? Good. Great stuff. You'd better go and get some sleep."

One business partner reporting on the ripeness of some jointly owned vineyard to another, except that Robert Hesketh was speaking from South Australia while Herrick was driving me towards their new winery in the Languedoc. La Motte is an old vin ordinaire farm on canalside flatlands just north of Narbonne where no self-respecting Frenchman would dream of trying to produce world-class wine, it being outside any of France's zealously-guarded zones for Appellation Contrôlée wines.

But, as I reported in the Weekend FT early in 1990, Global Vineyards' (sic) policy is to apply the snazzy techniques and unfettered philosophy of the New World to the relatively cheap vineyard land of southern France. I thought it would be interesting to spend a day with Herrick this spring, as the first of their 175 hectares (385 acres) of French Chardonnay were just starting to bear fruit, and I was right.

The Australians moved in by stealth over Christmas 1989 but now the Languedoc is abuzz with rumour and fact concerning outside investment. Château Ricardelle, a prominent property just south of Narbonne, is now being revitalised by a Swiss-Italian group. Peter Sichel and Bernadette Villars are just two of the Bordeaux proprietors who have already bought in Corbières (AC, of course) and a Belgo-Bordeaux group has moved into La Clape. On the way in to Narbonne Herrick had pointed out another rather handsome Corbières property that would apparently have been snapped up by another Bordelais had it not been for the financial predations of the last year's frosts.

We arrived at La Motte to a vineyard quite unlike its unkempt neighbours with their gnarled little straggly vine bushes dotting the bare earth. Here were carefully manicured rows of Chardonnay vines three grassy metres apart, the juicy leaves sprouting obediently and exclusively along wires at shoulder height, machine-tightened between posts that looked like cabers and unlike anything I'd seen in any other French vineyard.

"It's a system of moveable trellis wires designed to produce eight tones per acre, but here we're not allowed to make more than five," Herrick explained in the tone of indulgent exasperation he uses for France and the French. (When talking French to the French he uses no perceptible accent and a lot of self-deprecating grunts.)

Outside the old farm buildings, swarming with workmen and Radio Narbonne, was a British car and a truck carrying a warning against bushfires in the state of Victoria. English, or at least Strine, is the first language of most key employees here. Inside, 60 year-old concrete wine vats, through which a sea of once-profitable light red ordinaire has washed, are being sandblasted and re-lined ready to meet the requirements of an array of technically exacting New World wine-makers late this summer.

The South Australia winery Yalumba will be flying over a wine-maker, who in the southern hemisphere would be twiddling his thumbs at this time of year, to see what he makes of French fruit. Jacques and François Lurton, young brothers raised in Bordeaux but enologically schooled in Australia, will also be making wine here. And Global Vineyards itself plans to sell the first crop off its Chardonnay vines, spread over three different, unusually large domaines, to the huge Skalli operation in Sète and to fellow Australians Hardy's who bought a large winery outside Béziers two years ago.

As we leave we almost bump into a truck delivering the first consignment of this year's purchase of millions of metres of wire, an essential ingredient in imposing nurture rather than nature on the vines.

We pass a pretty farmhouse that is apparently being turned into gîtes by an English couple ("probably a far more sensible use of vineyard land" sighs Herrick). Next, the miserable sight of acres of ancient vines being properly ripped out, including all possible associated pests and diseases, by a team under Global Vineyards management. This is work for a neighbour who has been impressed by what les Australiens have done so far and plans to substitute modish Chardonnay vines for his old Carignan and Cinsault stumps.

Current EC subsidies ensure that it is more profitable to rip out a lacklustre old vineyard than to produce lacklustre wine for the local co-op from it. "But this guy actually wants to bottle the wine himself - a major step forward", says Herrick who reckons that the ill wind of phylloxera that has infected so many California vineyards might eventually just blow Global Vineyards and their vine-ripping expertise some good. "The trouble is that this vine pulling programme is artificially inflating the price of land here so that only the brave, foolish or wealthy can afford to invest in it."

We spend the rest of the day touring the properties of these brave, foolish or wealthy creatures. Jaques Ribourel is certainly the last of these, one of France's more successful real estate tycoons who seems perfectly happy to, literally, throw his millions into a large hole in the ground. He has heard that underground wineries are a good idea and so has had a vast 20 foot crater quarried out of the rock of La Clape mountain between Narbonne and the sea at an estimated cost of two million francs for the hole alone.

His Domaine de l'Hospitalet covers 1000 hectares (2,500 acres) but he doesn't like the shape of some of them so they are being remodelled too. His son Jeremie climbs down from his Paris-registered Range Rover to explain that eventually 22 vine varieties will be planted, plus a collection of local plants, a couple of outdoor theatres and lots, lots more, provided they can persuade plants to grow in the moonscape that is l'Hospitalet at present.

Next stop an established wine domain recently bought by someone who certainly qualifies as brave. Some idea of its size, and its output in the bad old days of quantity above quality, is given by the length of the winery building: 300 metres of wine vats at the very least.

Driving up an abandoned avenue towards the other buildings, which once included chapel, forge, workshops and school, Herrick makes disapproving noises about the dilapidated state of the vineyards. Local gossip has it that the new owner, a Champenois, paid for this 200 hectare property by selling two hectares of champagne vineyard.

As we dot about the rest of the region, each village eliciting another rumour about incoming investment, the temperature drops, the skies darken and so does Herrick's brow. There are still three more weeks during which those juicy little Chardonnay sprouts could be frozen and the less worldly locals, who can't understand why les Australiens are planting such an outlandish vine on low-lying land anyway, could be proved right.

As things turn out, it looks as though Global Vineyards (France) will at last have an entry on the credit side of the books this year, but it is undoubtedly operating in Europe's hottest viticultural melting pot.

June 13, 1992

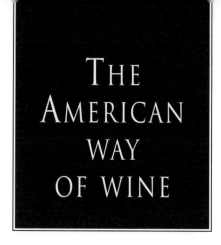

THE AMERICAN WAY OF WINE

I despair, I really do. There's that huge country across the Atlantic with its 200 million consumers not so very different from us Europeans, but how many of them are ever going to experience the true, and delightfully simple, pleasures of wine? Probably a handful at most unless there is a complete rotation of American mind-set on wine.

At the moment the wine that sells in America is either very cheap, very expensive, or regarded as a medicine. At the bottom end a shrinking proportion of the mass market buys basic commercial blends, with their persuasive sugar levels, and swigs them for refreshment as an alternative to a cola, with no more thought than they deserve. At the top end of the market a much smaller, static number of consumers, probably 0.1 per cent at most, are interested - and I mean passionately interested - in nothing but the very, very best and will pay any price to secure a case or two of it.

So well-heeled Americans gobble up the icing on the cake (helping to drive up its price) while the poor hoover up the crumbs, but Americans are effectively uninterested in the bread and butter of the wine world, the exciting variety of good-value bottles that can be enjoyed every day. Okay, some Americans will buy mid-range California wines in restaurants, but only because they resent paying restaurant mark-ups on the top wines they have in their cellars.

And they all agree which are the top wines because they all read The Wine Advocate newsletter and The Wine Spectator magazine which dispense, per wine, easily comprehensible scores out of 100; pocket calculators have replaced palates in the American wine trade. One New York restaurant, Zoe, even prints Spectator scores baldly on its wine list, with special sections for the 'heavy hitters' (scores over 90).

But a dangerously high proportion of wine in America is filling cellars rather than glasses. Wine connoisseurship has enjoyed a period of unparalleled status in the US. A cellarful of 90pointers has been seen as an essential accoutrement of success. The cellar will be specially constructed, its temperature and humidity carefully controlled, but its design is often predicated on its function as spectacle rather than store-cupboard. The bottles are for ogling rather than opening.

As one important Bordeaux merchant puts it, "the stock I'm worried about isn't sitting in Bordeaux; it's sitting in cellars all over America where its owner goes to look at it every weekend and comes back emptyhanded".

Bottles are sometimes opened, en masse, at grand, well-publicised tasting marathons at which perhaps 100 wines, each individually capable of sustaining a memorable dinner, are compared, and expectorated. But the proportion of great wine that is served as it is meant to be, a bottle or two at a time to maximise pleasure around a table, seems absurdly low from this side of the Atlantic. American for someone who takes an interest in wine is, significantly, not connoisseur or enthusiast but 'collector'.

There are those however who think that the only way wine will survive the activism of those labelled 'neo-Prohibitionists' is by becoming even more elitist. For years now, all wine bottles, even the grandest, must carry labels warning off pregnant women and those in charge of machinery. Increasing controls and some crazy litigation have wrought striking attitudinal changes in the American public.

A French wine merchant dining alone in a Boston steakhouse recently tried to sample a rival's brand, available only by the bottle. He was flabbergasted to have his order refused by a waitress who told him that a bottle was too much for one person and that she risked being held legally responsible for his actions if he consumed it. If the French wine trade were not in such dire straits at the moment, with Japan's second coming to wine looking increasingly mirage-like, one feels the French might be tempted to give up on the American market altogether.

Ever since Prohibition, selling any alcoholic liquid in the US has been notoriously complicated, with labrynthine but different rules for each state, but the hurdles placed between producer and US consumer seem to double each year. Perhaps symptomatic of wine's place in American society is that wine's chief regulatory body is the fiercely literal Bureau of Alcohol, Tobacco and Firearms.

The BATF must have been as shocked as the wine trade, if in a very different way, by the extraordinary television broadcast last November on CBS's '60 Minutes'. Morley Safer, a sort of Wogan-Dimbleby hybrid, told 30 million Americans of the research that suggests that one of the factors that keeps the French heart disease rate 40 per cent lower than in the US may be France's more robust consumption of red wine.

Who could have predicted such a boon for the wine trade from this unexpected quarter! Little old ladies teetered into liquor stores the very next morning asking for a bottle of that stuff that wards off heart attacks. My practically teetotal but cholesterol-fixated Californian friend manfully starting washing down his lunch with premier cru burgundy. Gallo, the world's largest winery, has had to put all of its reds, even its much-maligned jugs of 'Hearty Burgundy', on allocation only. Red wine sales immediately increased by more than 40 per cent.

But the American wine trade is trying desperately not to get too excited. Oat bran, sold a few years ago along much the same lines, proved more of a fling than a sustained love affair for the American public. It will not be in our lifetimes that Americans fall for the sort of relaxed life enhancement that regular consumption of good-value wine can offer.

July 4, 1992

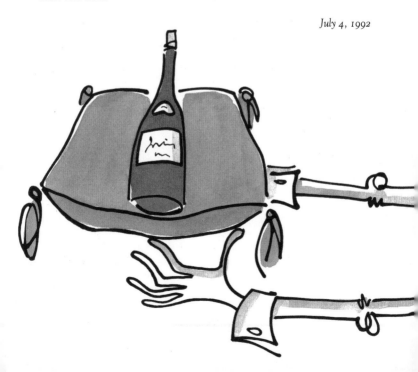

No no, AFTER YOU... OPUS ONE

aroness Philippine de Rothschild was half an hour late for our hour-long meeting, which is not bad going for her. And she did have a very good excuse. "It's so difficult for us women to get dressed in hotels!" she wailed as she sashayed in to one of the well-upholstered sitting rooms above London's Gavroche restaurant from her bedroom next door.

Her business partner 79 year-old Robert Mondavi, the biggest cheese in California wine, had got up in Paris at five that morning to be at this meeting and had arrived, via checking in at Claridge's, on the dot.

The two partners were in London to make a noise about their latest joint spending spree, on a splendiferously luxurious winery for their famous co-production Opus One, an ambitious red made from Napa Valley grapes to much the same recipe as firstgrowth bordeaux Ch Mouton-Rothschild. So how much did this new winery cost?

"Oooch. That's difficult to say," said Mondavi politely, before wandering off down several precious minutes' worth of conversational byways, taking in gravity flow, cement floors, basket presses... "Now," broke in the Baroness next to him, briskly stroking her dramatic black and white silk shift. "You asked about price and I think we should answer this because otherwise it sounds as though we don't want to talk about it, which is not the case. I would say $15 million."

"How much?" asked Mondavi, whose hearing is less keen than his forehand nowadays.

"I would say between 15 and 20 million dollars," beamed the ex-actress as Mondavi's legendary jaw dropped on to his chest. "Okay, it's a little bit less than the real cost," said the Baroness patting his knee, "but I'm sure, Jancis, you'll agree with me."

"I don't agree with you," muttered Mondavi from his corner of the sofa, before mustering a brave smile.

They make a great double act. Both with their own family-owned wine empires, each with a solid base of high-volume lines (Mouton-Cadet and inexpensive Central Valley bottlings respectively) providing the cashflow for their world-famous, high-cachet lines (Ch Mouton-Rothschild and Mondavi Napa Valley Reserve wines). They each have a 50 per cent stake in Opus One, originally devised as California's most expensive wine by the Baroness's late father Philippe, the most creative man the wine business has ever known. Philippine is confident enough today to describe it as "a crazy bet".

But like Mouton-Rothschild, Opus One is quintessentially finite. The winery has been lovingly sculpted to produce just 20,000 cases a year (rather less than the average production of Ch Mouton-Rothschild) which, even though Opus retails at around $65 a bottle, does rather obviously raise the question of when they expect this grandiose transatlantic pipedream to start making any money.

Much whistling and rueful laughter from both corners of the sofa. "I would say that...", Mondavi began.

"Can I answer that?" the Baroness asked, entirely superfluously. "Our grandchildren's generation, not before then."

A mock-horrified Mondavi accused Philippine of spreading such gloom "just to make this interesting", but if Opus One does reach profitability within 20 years, as it surely will, it will be faster than any Bordeaux château this century.

Twenty million dollars certainly sounds remarkably modest for a seven-year building project that involved not only the architects who built San Francisco's TransAmerica pyramid, but also a task described in the glamorous prospectus as 'landscape implementation', and the discovery halfway through of a thermal spring just under the site of the ageing cellar. (Although Philippine was at pains to point out that, for reasons of economy, she had nobly renounced having her own quarters incorporated into the winery plans.)

It was while telling me about all this that Mondavi first used the phrase "we didn't flinch", which was to come up several times subsequently. He talks as though what he's been through would have beaten many a lesser man, and admits that his financial advisors have done more than their fair share of flinching. (Imagine, for example, trying to find in northern California a cost-effective way of selling on 30,000 egg yolks, the residue of the annual filtration process that faithfully replicates Bordeaux practice.)

But for both parties Opus One is clearly a major project for the long term. Stuart Harrison, the outfit's sales and marketing director and in pre-winery times its only employee, surely has one of the world's easier jobs. Nowadays Opus One has merely to be allocated: three-quarters is snapped up in the first six weeks after release by America's well-primed collectors and the rest is carefully shared around the rest of the globe (just 150 cases for the entire United Kingdom, for example).

After my 30 breathless minutes with the two partners, I found myself sitting between Messrs Harrison and Mondavi comparing the extremely suave, definitively world-class 1987 Opus One with the much gawkier current vintage, 1988. Were these wines priced the same, I asked Mondavi. "I certainly hope not," he said, "let's ask Stu." The hapless Stu had to confess that, if anything, the younger wine was the more expensive. Mondavi was furious. "Now that's against everything I stood for!"

But Robert Mondavi (who is currently busy "looking at" Chile) is having to pay the price of handing over to his sons Tim and Michael. As chief winemaker, Tim makes the winemaking decisions about Opus One with Patrick Léon of Mouton, who was just one of 90 Rothschild employees and associates, some of whom had never left Pauillac, flown over to California at the end of last May to see just what all that money had been diverted to.

The 1991 vintage was the first to be made at the new winery, as opposed to the Mondavi winery across Highway 29, and rumour has it that it will be one of the greats. For my money - or rather yours since I'm so unsophisticated I want a bordeaux first-growth if I'm paying a bordeaux first-growth price - the best vintages so far have been the 1982, 1985 and 1987. Adnams of Southwold list the 1985, drinking spendidly now, for £46.50 a bottle, and some branches of Davisons around London have the 1987 for £37.25.

July 11, 1992

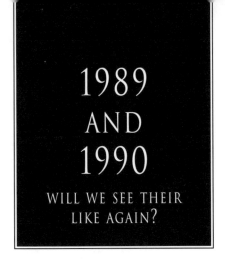

1989 AND 1990

WILL WE SEE THEIR LIKE AGAIN?

Great vintages, like Robert Maxwell and punk, need some sort of historical perspective before their true worth can be assessed. But since so many of the best wines are on the market only in their infancy, wine buyers have traditionally had to take a foreshortened view if they are not to be left wishing they had, instead of gloating over what they have.

At the moment we should be gazing up in wonder at the magnificence of the 1989 and 1990 vintages in Europe and working out just how many cases we can afford of this extraordinary double-act - and we all thought 1988 was pretty good at the time too.

This is certainly true of the great sweet whites of Bordeaux, the Loire, Alsace, Germany - and indeed of the much-widened spectrum of German wines now available. The exceptional ripeness of 1989 and 1990 made some wonderfully exuberant drier German wines too, particularly from the stars of the Rheinpfalz, Lingenfelder and Müller-Catoir whose essence-like whites are marvels of concentration, whether dry (Trocken), medium dry (Halbtrocken) or unreined. Both producers' wines are sold by Oddbins whose greatest bargain has been Müller-Catoir's last (1990) vintage of Müller-Thurgau (£4.99) makes one revise all assumptions about this workaday grape variety. But even wines at the top of this glorious range, which should continue to develop for a decade or two, cost less than £10.

In France 1989 and 1990 were also exceptional for reds at the exalted level of the smartest burgundies and (less rare) classed growth claret, but also in each of the Loire, the Rhône and the Midi where 1990 in particular was a smash hit.

In the Loire, these two great vintages arrived just as a decent proportion of producers had got to grips with making serious sweet white wines without recourse to added sugar and sulphur, and had mastered the vigour of their vines to ripen red grapes fully. This has resulted not only in some fabulous (no overstatement) sweet Vouvrays (for Huet, try Bibendum, London NW1 and The Wine Society of Stevenage) but also in a range of gorgeous reds with more lush fruit than I have ever come across from the Loire. Britain's greatest range of seriously good Loire wines of all hues is on the wholesale list of the restaurant RSJ in London SE1 (0171-928 4554), an enclave of Loiromania, but you have to buy by the dozen.

August 1, 1992

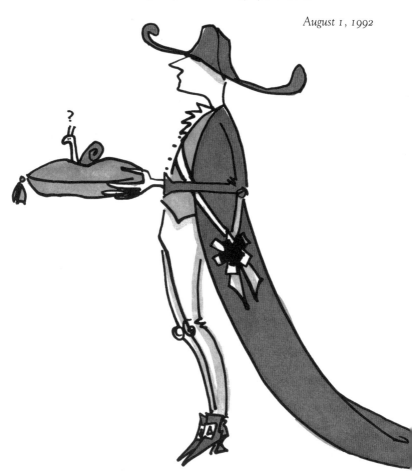

FRATERNITIES OF THE FRYING PAN

Those who missed a trip to France this summer, panicked perhaps by blocked autoroutes or drained finances, could experience much of the essential Frenchness of France for £35, the price of a new privately-published guide to one of the country's identifying institutions, 'Les Grandes Confréries de France'. These confréries are true brotherhoods, built not on personal commercial advancement but on greed of a purer sort. Although ritual is crucial to the 150-odd brotherhoods lovingly detailed in the book, their unifying theme is not masonic but, perhaps not surprisingly, gastronomic. No wine is too obscure, no victual too mundane, no sweetmeat too slight to have an entire constitution, chapter of officers and roster of ceremonies centred on it. Here are Confréries dedicated to quince jam, choucroute, Cavaillon melon, pheasant terrine, tripes â la mode fertoise, the famous red wine of Ottrott and the white (I think) of Noble-Joue of which I was equally, if shamefully, ignorant before discovering this new index of epicurean devotions.

The Confrérie exists to promulgate by gathering, and the typical gathering is a long ceremony during which new members are 'intronised' to an honorary rank and formally required to eat, drink, identify or swear eternal allegiance to the comestible in question, followed by an even longer, and much more convivial, feast.

In a small village outside Albi, for instance, is the Order of the Stuffed Chicken, whose male members attain the rank of Coq et Chevalier, females that of Coquette Dame. The mirabelle plum of Lorraine has been defended by its own 'Consultat' since 1974, the pumpkin paté of Millancay only since 1980 while the sausage of Muscadet was left to fend for itself until May 1990. Even the art of slashing the top off a champagne bottle with a sabre has its very own Confrérie du Sabre d'Or.

The author and publisher of this heroic and revealing work is Bernard Tardif, himself President and Grandmaster of the Confrérie

Gastronomique de la Marmite d'Or (golden stewpot), a sort of National Trust of the French table, having resurrected an ancient royal company of provisioners nearly two centuries after Robespierre sentenced it to an extended siesta. His book is not cheap and one ponders at first the luxury of printing at least one full-colour photograph on most of its 250 pages. But this is to overlook another vital aspect of life as a Confrère, the clothes. The French more than anyone believe the maxim that you haven't done it if you haven't dressed for it (*vide* any possible route for France's weekend cyclists) and this book provides glorious, nay sumptuous, proof of the French robe-maker's ingenuity. Each order has not only its own ranks, certificates and traditions, but its own uniform, designed to add pomp to what might otherwise, just possibly, look a little silly.

The robe should ideally be floor-length, generous in cut (especially round the girth), vaguely evoke medieval heraldry (and if possible the product in question), incorporate a sash and/or clanking insignia and, of course, a hat. Typical, and dashed smart, is the uniform of the Chevaliers de l'Olivier, based at Nyons in the southern Rhône. Their velvet cloaks with matching olive-sprigged trilbys are, of course, in olive green (the regulation red bow tie surely not representing a pimento stuffing?), but the rigout must be jolly hot at their regular meeting on the first Sunday of July. One of the most fetching costumes is the emerald and shocking pink satin smock and bakers' bonnet worn by the Confrérie of the Saulxures raspberry, founded back in 1972. The brilliant orange robes and green striped headgear designed to celebrate the Cormery macaroon on the other hand look as though they had just been unpacked for the photographer, but then this Confrérie was only founded in 1990.

This is not at all like the seriously charitable, and seminal, Jurade de St-Emilion to which I have the honour of belonging (as Dame) along with the Commanderie du Bontemps du Médoc et Graves, the grand order of the burgundian snail (which, worryingly, does not feature in this book but then I was told when I joined back in 1977 that France already imported most its snails from Taiwan), and the noble order of the trou normand (or mid-meal shot of calvados). The oldest of France's confreries, the Jurade can trace its roots back to 1199 and is based, like all of Confreriedom, on a charter governing the administration of a part of France then under the English crown. So it is possible that without us, French life (and presumably Monsieur Tardif) would be considerably the poorer.

Les Grandes Confreries de France' is available only by mail from Bernard Tardif, 5 Allée de la Chevaleries, 37170 Chambray-lès-Tours, France. FF 315 inc postage.

September 5, 1992

A LANGUEDOC-ROUSSILLON PRIMER

We all know that France's biggest wine region can now offer some of the world's best value bottles but few of us, even wine merchants and wine writers, know our way round it yet. Britain's biggest off-licence chain thinks Sète is "on the edge of Cotes de Rousillon(sic)", most of its rivals still lump both Languedoc and Roussillon in with minor obscurities under the belittling title French Country Wines, and many wonder where Oc is. Herewith the briefest of bluffers' guides to bottles that can offer real diversity and character in the £3 to £5 bracket:

MIDI is a general but delightfully evocative name for the south of France. In terms of time rather than place, midi is noon, a time of firmly closed shutters when you may as well have your feet under a table here as everyone else will be busy lunching or snoozing.

LANGUEDOC, the land where "*oc*" meant yes and white wine is still pronounced "*venga blenga*", is a vast sweep of vine monoculture around the Mediterranean coast. Generalisations about the wines produced are now, happily, impossible. The plains which once spewed forth vapid vin ordinaire for thirsty workers in northern France now boast pockets of quality-consciousness where prices are still ludicrously low (which means most cellars are still frugally equipped). In modern times the Languedoc has been divided up into, from east to west, the Gard, Hérault and Aude departements, each of which have their own Vins de Pays (see below).

ROUSSILLON should not be a Languedoc suffix at all but is the quite distinct, Pyreneen, semi-Spanish region that is French Catalonia. Here are exotic soft, full, dry whites; some uniquely complex dessert wines labelled Banyuls, Maury and Rivesaltes; and reds that are cheap but only occasionally excite. The Rivesaltes co-operative and the larger houses Cazes and Sarda-Malet do a good job but all producers struggle to fit the wines they want to make into the straitjacket of appellation contrôlée rules.

CORBIERES The Languedoc's most interesting appellation, spread over 11 newly-defined but almost equally rugged terroirs of arid, generally hilly vineyards. Although generic blends of Corbières are as dull as any, many individual domaines are busting a gut to win medals and competitions with wines as well-made as France's finest. A typical good Corbières is deep red, slightly wild and intensely savoury. Fine dry whites are also increasingly easy to find, if not invariably thanks to fashions for oak-ageing and grape varieties as exotic as Roussanne, Marsanne, Vermentino and even Viognier. Over-achievers: Lastours, Voulte-Gasparets (Cuvée Romain Pauc), Roque-Sestière (white), St Auriol, La Baronne, Villemajou, Fontsainte, Ollieux.

MINERVOIS is the queen if Corbières is king, its wines lacking some of the punch perhaps, but making up for it with their suavity. As in Corbières, the best reds are made of Syrah, Grenache, Cinsault, Mourvèdre and as little Carignan as possible. Here too there are dozens of dedicated domaines, but also some fine co-operatives which are investing in such luxuries as de-stalking machines and new oak casks. Over-achievers: Fabas, Laville-Bertrou, Fontbertière, La Combe Blanche, Violet, Gourgazaud, Centeilles, La Grave, Tour St Martin, Jean d'Alibert.

FITOU commands a mysterious price premium over the two appellations above which lie to its immediate north, but has recently been coasting on a reputation cleverly built upon the wholesome-sounding but effectively fictitious Madame Parmentier's label. At best a mature Fitou can be a rewarding, fullblown experience but too high a proportion of production is undistinguished, fairly tough, high-volume stuff. Notable exception: Ch de Nouvelles.

ST CHINIAN, the appellation to the immediate east of Minervois, is already slightly more Rhône-like, producing rounder red, and occasionally pink, wines with more obvious Cinsaut/Grenache sweetness, which can make them slightly less distinctive to palates brought up on Côtes-du-Rhône. Over-achievers: Coujan, Jougla, Berloup (top cuvées).

FAUGERES The best are silkier than St Chinian next door and manage to slip the juiciness of the local grape varieties into a bordeaux-like structure. Over-achievers: Estanilles, Laurens, Grezan.

COTEAUX DU LANGUEDOC is the catch-all appellation for wines made east of Minervois and west of the Gard of which the authorities approve (i.e. are not named after grape varieties). So far subregions St Chinian and Faugères have managed to float above the surface to establish their own identity. Others bubbling up include La Clape whose Bourboulenc whites can beguile, another white oddity Picpoul de Pinet, and Pic St Loup. Over-achievers: Rouquette-sur-Mer (white), Mas Jullien, Prieure de St Jean de Bebian, Hortus (stunning red).

VIN DE PAYS Most of France's 'country wines' come from either the Languedoc or Roussillon, and many of the Languedoc-Roussillon's most interesting wines qualify only as Vin de Pays rather than one of the appellations above. They often carry obscure geographical names, but can offer superb value. The most common is the catch-all Languedoc category, Vin de Pays d'Oc, which may also be labelled with the name of a grape variety. Syrah and Merlot have been particularly successful reds, while whites stray boldly outside Chardonnay and Sauvignon territory.

Although Chardonnay is being planted fast and furiously, until recently the lion's share of Languedoc Chardonnay was planted around Limoux, famous for its sparkling Blanquette. After Mas de Daumas Gassac, the Vin de Pays de l'Hérault with the classed growth prices, the most successful PR coup has been Limoux coop's Toques et Clochers annual auction of oak-aged Chardonnays, now available from Britain's Majestic chain for around £7.50.

Some of Roussillon's finest wines qualify only as Vin de Pays (and Fernand Vaquer's only as Vin de Table) because of grape varieties or alcohol levels. Languedoc: Condamine l'Eveque, Limbardie, Arjolle, St Martin de la Garrigue, Aupilhac, Bosc/Cante Cigale, Valmagne, Raissac, Peyrat, Montmarin, Coussergues. Roussillon: Mas Chichet, Gauby, Cazenove.

MUSCATS abound but best value, if smallest, golden sweet wine appellation is St Jean de Minervois.

September 26, 1992

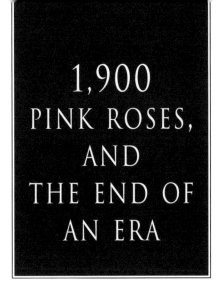

1,900 PINK ROSES, AND THE END OF AN ERA

Towards the end of the night Lalou Bize-Leroy confessed it would be her last September Tasting. The last time she would spend a week preparing her sumptous Burgundian farmhouse for its annual influx of the great and the good in the wine buying and wine writing worlds. Every September since 1964 they have climbed the hills above Meursault in their Mercedes and Porsches to be ritually humiliated.

Many of the world's more reputable wine tasters will sleep easier now, safe in the knowledge that never again will they have to participate in this famous blind tasting competition, although the wines were so good that it always seemed worth running the risk of making a fool of oneself. This year, for example, we were served 33 different vintages of the great red burgundy, Le Chambertin itself, back to 1933. All we had to do, as mystery glass after glass washed over us, was say which year was which.

Lalou, as we all call her as though she were our intimate, is probably the wine world's most famous woman, most famous at the moment for a bitter, public and extremely expensive dispute with her ex-business partner and her sister. But she is famous for far more than being the ex-co-director of the fabulous Domaine de la Romanée-Conti who has so infuriatingly set up her own rival Domaine Leroy along the village backstreets of Vosne-Romanée.

An awesome, and unusually glamorous, taster, she is passionate about her wines, and now vines, almost to the point of clinical mania.

The grapes that arrive at her newly equipped winery are treated, as she says herself, like the most tender strawberries. Showing me six men poring over the slowest sorting belt, the shallow trays in which the grapes are transported, the holes deliberately punched so that any excess moisture simply runs away, the serried ranks of brand new wooden vats and the specially-designed cruising metal substitute for the more brutal human foot, she asked helplessly, "surely any *Financial Times* reader would be horrified by the craziness of this sort of investment?" (around £8 million to make hardly 7,000 cases of wine a year).

In the perfectly-kept cellars below, French wine oracle Michel Bettane and I are taken on a cask-by-cask tour of the 1991 vintage. Thanks to her fastidiousness, and her gifted and compliant winemaker André Porcheret, they are marvels of geographical expression. But even in the one or two cases where we express the minutest reservation, we are corrected. No mother is more besotted.

In the great Richebourg vineyard we are asked to marvel at the smallness, ripeness, paucity, upright stance of her 'biodynamic' grapes - especially in comparison with those of a particularly famous holding next door... This is a woman whose idea of relaxation is to pit her tiny frame against a rockface.

The stated purpose of her September Tastings is to make her guests taste great burgundy with due attention, but it hasn't always felt like that. Lalou, in Chanel or perhaps Lacroix, welcomes her guests outside with a glass of mystery white, her stilettos crunching the gravel that separates her stone farmhouse from the ancient trees encircling it. In 1988, my initiation year, guests included Bocuse the chef, Broadbent the auctioneer, Duboeuf the Beaujolais, Domecq the sherry, Wasserman the broker as well as a host of collectors and writers from both sides of the Atlantic. This year instead there was a significant Japanese presence - hardly surprising since Lalou's important new vineyard acquisitions have been heavily financed by her Japanese agents Takashimaya (a name she still has difficulty spelling).

Eventually we take our places inside where sideboards are already charged with the lobsters, ecrevisses, wild rice, pâtés, sweetbreads and sweetmeats that have been pouring out of Lalou's kitchen over the last few days. (Hers is surely the only table in France where truffles are easier to find than bread.) Yet another perennial distraction from the dozens of mystery wines to come has been a heady array of flowers, this year no fewer than 1,900 pink roses in that perfect state between bud and bloom.

But the most daunting aspect of the tasting is that each of the 50 or 60 guests, many of them senior figures in the world of wine, is given a beautifully printed little notebook, from which we have to hand in to Miss (our eagle-eyed hostess) a page of our guesses for each flight of wines. "One point will be given to each correct response", it says, and sure enough the denouement of each September Tasting has been the announcement of the 'winner'. The late Jean Troisgros usually managed more points than most, but an outsider would probably be appalled by how few points are actually scored.

Lalou may patrol the room declaiming the obviousness of various wines but as Michael Broadbent of Christie's, author of several wine tasting bibles, freely admits, "I always make an absolute balls of it". Michel Bettane, who has occasionally been top scorer, managed just four points out of 40 one year, as did Matt Kramer, author of 'Making Sense of Burgundy'. This year's winner, Lalou's all-important American importer Martine Saunier, identified 11 vintages out of the 33 for example.

We shall all miss our annual humbling. In fact the whole equilibrium of Burgundy seems upset by what has already been a financial humbling for Lalou, who has lost the lucrative rights to sell Domaine de la Romanée-Conti wines (which used to account for three-quarters of Leroy's turnover). In its vast and sepulchral warehouses in Auxey-Duresses, the old negociant business of Leroy still holds millions of pounds' worth of the older vintages Lalou used to buy in before turning vigneronne. (She had been hoping that American guru Robert Parker would come to her tasting this year and move a bit of stock by writing nice things about those venerable Chambertins.)

She says that in future years she may hold some sort of tasting not at home but at the new Domaine Leroy in Vosne-Romanée. It should certainly be exposed to as many wine drinkers as possible, as a shrine to single-mindedness.

October 3, 1992

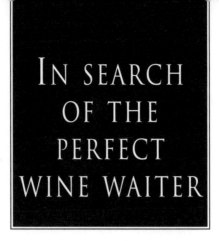

IN SEARCH OF THE PERFECT WINE WAITER

I n the old days the perfect wine waiter was just like the stereotype wine waiter - Francocentric, heavily accented, impenetrably aloof, his role to reduce customers to Bateman cartoon fodder with the drop of an eyelid. Except that the best did actually know something about wine.

But just as wines have been changing, so have restaurants and their customers, and there is now an entirely new breed of wine waiter. These guys, just for starters, may not even be guys. But whether male or female, they will almost invariably be young, enthusiastic, knowledgeable in a truly international sense, and completely, almost unsettlingly, unfettered by tradition. Fishcakes with Cabernet? You got it. Cloudy Bay with Chili? You got it. Etcetera.

So what does make the perfect wine waiter nowadays? He, or she, has to combine a pleasant modesty with flexibility. He has to satisfy the everyday, non-wine-fanatic customer by reliably recommending good buys at the cheaper end of the list. But he also has to be able to hold his own with the increasing number of wine maniacs who now roam the world and enjoy torturing sommeliers with tricky questions and absurd boasts. He has to satisfy his employer by generating sufficient profit from the declining number of bottles ordered, especially at lunchtime. And finally, so that he can be fielded at any time for the role of wine waiter in a sitcom, he should ideally have a strong French accent and an Inspector Clouseau moustache.

I know the very chap. Gérard Basset, currently posing as a Frenchman working (extremely hard) at Hampshire's famous country house hotel, Chewton Glen. So perfect is he that he has just, very nearly, been voted the Best Sommelier in the World. At what are effectively the sommelier Olympics, held every three years, Gérard Basset was beaten into second place by one point, by talented Philippe Faure-Brac of Paris. Faure-Brac is very French, and is expected to make as much of his new title as his countryman who won it back in 1983 and has virtually built a business empire on it.

But Basset surely cannot be French. Quite apart from his natural modesty and caricature French accent, there is what he says. For example: "England is fantastic - a far better place to learn about wine than France. The more I learn, the more I realise I don't know. A lot of sommeliers forget to respect the customer. The only customers I'm not overkeen on are the French. I used to try to sell them wines from new regions such as California. Now I say, 'Unless you're open-minded, don't bother'."

Perhaps on the other hand, he really was born in St Etienne (fork left for Côtes du Forez) in 1957 and fell in love with England via a football match in Liverpool, unlikely as this may seem. Other talented French sommeliers have deliberately chosen to make British hotels such as the Manoir, the Inn on the Park, the London Intercontinental and the Lanesborough their base for learning about wine, because the chances to learn about nonFrench wines are so much greater (even if the matching of specific wines and foods is largely ignored).

Certainly the World Sommelier Championship, held this year in Brazil, requires truly non chauvinist wine knowledge. The questions Gérard can remember from the written exam on the Friday included pairing the names of 10 of Italy's arcane Supertuscans with their producers, and ranged from California wine nomenclature, through the Luxembourg appellation system to the role of vitamins in grapes. The practical part of this qualifying round involved serving a Brazilian Cabernet Sauvignon correctly.

This reduced the 35 finalists to five who had to perform in public on the Saturday, describing and recommending wines (and spirits) from an 800-bin list they had only half an hour to study, and answering such nasty questions as "What do you think of Michel Lynch 1986?" (Some contestants were so nervous they managed to stumble out an appreciation of this wine, which did not exist at that time.)

Basset is lucky. Both his employers at Chewton Glen and his fiancée Nina Howe (an AA hotel inspector) actively support his dedication to a series of vinous title fights. Priestlike, he studies theory religiously each morning before going off to further his practical mastery of wine waiting.

His next ambition is to pass the Master of Wine exams, the highest academic qualification in the wine trade, which he describes with some relish as a marathon compared to the 'sprint' in Brazil. Nina will continue to test him with mystery glasses served during their two evenings a week together, since the MW also involves practical as well as theoretical exams. And they have advertised in the local paper for someone to coach him in the necessary essay writing.

He says rather touchingly that his overall aim is to motivate others to become sommeliers by helping to change their arrogant image. "But you know," he said conspiratorially, "the worst are some of my young French staff. One of them, a 19 year-old, told me off the other day for decanting a Pinot Noir. So I waited until after service and asked him to explain exactly why I shouldn't. And do you know the only reason he could give me? Because 'in France we don't'."

October 31, 1992

Gérard Basset left Chewton Glen in 1994 and is now installed at the Hotel du Vin, Winchester.

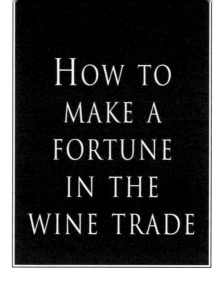

HOW TO MAKE A FORTUNE IN THE WINE TRADE

Lunch was served under a tree by the pool, the escargots and the duck cooked by the local two-star chef and smilingly served by his mother. In the dappled September sunlight of a good Burgundy vintage we watched two young men fulfil their pool maintenance contract and discussed the world's financial crisis.

The cold hand of stagnation and bankruptcy has certainly touched most parts of the wine business, but my hosts' very particular sector of it seems as hot as ever. Jean and Noelle François report little slackening of demand for the top quality French oak barrels they sell from their three pre-eminent cooperages: François Frères in Burgundy, Demptos just outside Bordeaux and Demptos Napa, a joint venture in California. Total production is more than 200 casks a day (75 in St Romain, 100 in Bordeaux, 30 in Napa) which can sell for well over £250 apiece. As Gérard Lebrère of their great rival, the biggest cooper Seguin Moreau, says happily, "the world is infatuated with new oak at the moment".

As more and more wine producers console themselves for slow demand with the mantra 'less but better', the wooden cask has taken on a mythic significance. At the lower end of the ladder the most obvious way a producer can jack up the price of his wine is to age it in wood, preferably oak new enough to impart a perceptible layer of 'oaky' flavour, and trumpet the fact on the label. At the top end, the increasingly high proportion of meticulously nurtured fruit in many cases demands meticulously coopered wood which not only adds more complex flavours but smooths the winemaking process. High scores and public acclaim are imperative to generate sales and top quality new French oak seems, at present anyway, to be the key.

Demand for oak casks is strong therefore from producers at the bottom who wish to climb and from those at the top who dare not slip. Only those producers with a real cash flow problem - such as Burgundy's logjammed negociants and smaller, mid-range domaines - have dramatically cut their orders for the 1992 vintage. But producers in the New World and emerging Old World wine regions who wish to demonstrate that they too belong to the wine world elite have more than compensated.

Of the 200,000 French oak barrels made for a particularly generous vintage such as 1990, more than half are exported, with the ambitious and relatively cash-rich wineries of California taking about half of all exports. The geographical diversification of the French cooperage business, initially impelled by the 1973 oil crisis, means that it is now, thanks to southern hemisphere orders, a year-round rather than three-month activity.

Survival in the cooperage business takes considerable nerve however, as well as financial reserves, which is why many smaller coopers have foundered. While not being so long-term as the timber business (trees should be at least a century old before being hewn into wine casks), a good cooper has to bet on his likely sales in two to three years' time, buying ahead after careful selection from France's efficiently-managed forests, which cover a quarter of that sizeable *hexagone*. Top quality oak tends to be from slow-growing trees from certain treasured areas, carefully split into staves by following the grain and then left outside for a couple of years like giant stacks of matches to yield the harshest tannins to the elements and the ground beneath. A stereotype cost-cutting barrel would be made from sawn staves, dried much faster over a kiln and possibly even assembled using glue rather than fire (to soften the staves) and sweat (to shape them into the hoops).

This relatively buoyant market is fought over by the 30 or so specialist coopers left in France, other than those well-heeled, traditional wine producers who still have their own in-house cooper. Three of the biggest are based in Cognac where barrels are all-important, but it is a sign of the relative health of the wine and brandy markets that Seguin Moreau is now a nice little earner for the Remy Martin group by selling 95 per cent of its barrels to wine producers. Taransaud uses its particularly fine stock of French oak to do the same for the Hennessy bit of the LVMH group while Vicard and Radoux are still independent. François Frères of Burgundy became the biggest family-run cooperage business in 1989 with their trans-hexagon acquisition of Demptos, to which Seguin Moreau have responded by setting up shop in Burgundy last November (although they already had offices in California and Australia). Nadallier is the other sizeable Bordeaux cooper.

Coopers such as Demptos will export staves for reconstruction into casks abroad but others try to minimise such potentially expensive problems as contamination and leaks by exporting whole made-up barrels sheathed in plastic. Like most craftsmen however, with the possible exception of chefs and marblers, coopers, as in those who actually coop for a living, are a disappearing species. Seguin Moreau have cleverly harnessed Portuguese cooperage skills to make up French staves.

Just as port and traditionally-matured Portuguese wines have kept the cooper's art alive in Portugal, so sherry, rioja and a wide range of wood-matured spirits mean that there are still flourishing cooperages in Spain, Scotland, Ireland and, particularly, America where bourbon must be matured in a new charred American oak cask. This rule, surely formulated by some American timber merchant, can generate sales of up to a million casks a year, many of which eventually find their way to Scotland where Scotch whisky producers are becoming increasingly worried by the possible effects of the bourbon slump on their own production costs. The future may bring new American oak casks. (Used wine casks tend to be traded down for use on increasingly lowly wines.)

The sherry producers of Andalucia play an important part in the cooperage business too, not just by breaking in oak casks specially for some of the more particular malt whisky producers, but by usefully abhorring new oak and using individual casks for up to 200 years. The sweeter, more obvious flavours of American oak have traditionally been favoured by Spanish wine and brandy producers ever since the seventeenth century, and this naturally less porous oak is also widely used for reds hefty enough to take it in Australia as well as California.

European oak is finer though and although there is no shortage of French oak, it is expensive, representing about half the price of a barrel today. Many coopers, mindful of history, are now looking east for cheaper oaks - particularly since there are, for the moment at least, few controls on exact wood provenance, however much Napa Valley winemakers agonise over whether to order Allier or Nevers - which names may in reality be used interchangeably by France's still blessed barrel salesmen.

November 7, 1992

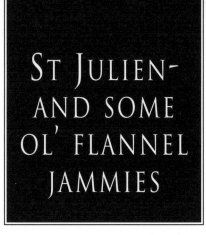

ST JULIEN-
AND SOME
OL' FLANNEL
JAMMIES

How many times have you heard it said that there's a world glut of fine wine? Forth Worth's Marvin C Overton III MD and his ilk have a solution. The problem is, you see, that we're all just too slow on the draw; our corkscrews spend far too long in the holster. If only we'd loosen up, get popping and match Overton's opening rate of nearly 20 bottles an hour, the planet's fine wine backlog could be cleared within months.

I couldn't believe the program he faxed me of a tasting I took myself off to co-host at the Four Seasons restaurant in New York last May. We were to begin at 9.30 in the morning apparently with 'Lillet over ice with a slice of orange', a glass of vermouth being just what you feel like after breakfast, especially with a total of 87 clarets in prospect.

Between 10 and an early lunch we were to taste 24 vintages of Ch Gloria plus 19 of Ch St Pierre. After lunch (just four wines with consomme and risotto), corks were pulled on no fewer than 40 vintages of Ch Ducru-Beaucaillou, three of them from the last century.

In the months before the event I had protested vigorously, twice, at this unseemly massacre. Do we really have to taste every vintage of the 1970s and 1980s, I bleated from my fax machine. Overton insisted from his: "The poor vintages are now not likely to show that well and are simply there for completeness to accentuate the true beauty of the better years. Do not be concerned. I have done this on any number of occasions and have it down pat."

And he did. By 12.15 we had raced through 43 red bordeaux - most of us having given the Lillet a miss, however much it may assist the fortunes of the Borie family of Ducru-Beaucaillou. Just before we got down to business the owner of second growth Ch Léoville-Barton pointedly remarked to the owner of Chx St Pierre (fourth growth) and Gloria (a mere cru bourgeois), "I should think you'll need a glass of Lillet before a tasting of Gloria". But at least he was there for it. The other second growth proprietor Jean-Eugène Borie of Ch Ducru-Beaucaillou did not appear until lunch. (The Bordelais were somewhat mystified by this flesh-free midday snack, one of them dismissing the modish wild mushroom risotto as "porridge".)

This gaggle of proprietors had one more thing in common: their properties are all in the same Bordeaux parish and, as Dr Overton put it in his opening remarks to the assembled wine collectors and writers, "We're not here to critique the wines, we're here to celebrate God's glorious place, St Julien".

Overton is unmistakeably Texan, not just for his bowlegged drawl but for his height, his apple cheeks, his resolute beam and his extraordinary taste in suits. I have to say that I found his jacket, sculpted by a famous Italian tailor from finest pinstripe to Dr Overton's own design incorporating a pointed cowboy yoke, almost as riveting as the Ducru 1867.

But perhaps what most distinguishes him as a Lone Star Statesman is the sheer scale of his ambition. All those bottles emptied, followed by a 15-wine dinner that night illuminated, natch, by his 20-minute home movie about St Julien ("and don't none of you laugh at ma French accent") - and this was just the start of his five-city, 10-château tour of the United States putting God's glorious place on the American wine collectors' map.

He is quite right to bring to their often blinkered attention that there is life beyond the first growths (St Julien has no first growth but is stuffed with exceptionally good seconds and others), but who else could possibly have imagined that they would be happy to board a 9 a.m. plane to Chicago the next day with 102 wines still sloshing around the bloodstream?

Overton, a neurological surgeon, clearly has heartening faith in the human body's ability to withstand the ravages of alcohol. "Ah farned ah have to let it all wash down mah throat. But it's just a liddle pour, it doesn't affect me," he confided, just before trying to wind up the event 13 vintages too early.

I spent the afternoon, doggedly trying to spit and write notes, flanked by the non-spitting Overton and the non-note-taking Borie whose grin became increasingly bemused. "I never had such a tasting. Marvin is always so active," beamed the proprietor of Ch Ducru-Beaucaillou. "At the château we have four bottles or so of the very old vintages, but none of this marvellous 1924. I'm going to try and buy some." As we tasted his surprisingly delightful 1969 he looked at it dolefully. "I never taste the 1969. I don't know - when I was young, I thought it wasn't very interesting to keep it for long."

The wines had come from a variety of sources - Overton's own cellar and those of fellow American collectors in particular although importers helped with newer vintages and the Ducru 1929 had been air freighted in from a London trader only that morning.

Overton, who loves organising these tasting marathons, is not only long on wine, but long on wine homilies, as in, "Ah always say that for the first 10 years of its life you have to work at a wine. For the second 10 years you marvel at it, and for the third 10 years you just let it float over you like yer ol' flannel jammies."

All over New York that week I kept bumping into wine folk asking "Why is he doing it?". I suppose it might have been to hear someone like Jean-Eugène Borie stand up after dinner at the Four Seasons and say "Marvin, you are very, very fantastic." But I think it was probably just ol' Marv doing his bit to deplete stocks, fast.

November 21, 1992

To my knowledge, Mr Overton has abandoned wine for a more ascetic sort of religion.

St. Julien.

HONOUR AND DISHONOUR IN OPORTO

I had felt so flattered to be asked to be the first woman to attend, and speak at, the annual Treasurer's Dinner at the Factory House in Oporto. The Factory House is somewhere very special, a handsome eighteenth century edifice on a patch of British soil in the middle of Portugal's second city, a relic of the days in which British merchants, or factors, needed a place to congregate and, doubtless, lament the lack of home comforts.

At one time these factors would have dealt in all sorts of commodities, but for nearly 200 years the Factory House in Oporto has been the seat of the Port Wine Trade, defined by their Britishness, their love of capital letters and their exclusion of women from their British Association and its weekly Wednesday Lunches.

This year it was the turn of port shippers Taylor to field a Treasurer, and his turn therefore to choose a speaker for the annual Treasurer's Dinner. In retrospect I suspect I was invited because the head of Taylor's, Alistair Robertson, has no sons but three daughters, and a wife who feels strongly about women and the Factory House. It was probably hoped that I would behave nicely and demonstrate that no evil would result from giving in to the inexorable dual-gender sweep of evolution (especially as an increasing number of women now play a serious part in the port business, the clever little things).

I certainly intended to behave myself. I purposely left in my wardrobe any remotely daring female answer to the Black Tie and, as I mounted the granite steps to the Factory House's first floor Drawing Room with its portraits of Grahams, Sandemans, Crofts, Warres and Symingtons, was absolutely determined to be as unembarrassingly inobtrusive as possible.

After rations of white port from golden decanters, 28 descendants of these Sandemans, Grahams etc and their workmates (some of them actually Portuguese), the British Ambassador, the incumbent of the British Church in Oporto and I made our way to the Dining Room. The bit in the Dining Room was fine. We chatted our way through a five-course dinner with a white Portuguese table wine, Camarate 1991, Ch Beychevelle 1984 ("hope you approve") and a 30 year-old tawny port.

There was a very slight hiccup as we got up to move to the same places at the table in the near-identical Dessert Room next door, a tradition as old as the long Georgian tables themselves. Should the lady go first? (No. Frightfully complicated. We'd never find our places in the candlelight.) It was here, over fruit and nuts and beautiful decanters in strictly clockwise motion, that we were to get down to the business of listening to the speeches and polishing off (11 bottles of) 'proper' port, Vintage Port, Taylor 1948 no less - an absolute dream of mellow concentration.

Did I say mellow? Well the shippers certainly showed signs of concentration on my speech, but I'm not sure that it left them feeling at all mellow. I had done my research on previous speakers and, realising I could hardly follow the jokey route of Willie Rushton, or the historical tour d'horizon of an ambassador, decided I'd better tell them about one of the few relevant things I probably knew a bit more about than they did: port and the British wine market, the one they depend on for sales of better quality ports, and profits.

I had honestly assumed that, before suggesting a few ways in which they might improve port's appeal, I would merely be illuminating some of the darker corners of a not particularly bright picture. After all, they must have noticed that port shipments to Britain, and to most other major markets, have been falling. But I felt as though my report on the portlessness of so much of contemporary British society came as an absolute bolt from the blue to this coterie of expatriates.

Before flying out to Oporto, I had done a certain amount of ringing round to discover just how much port was served where. To my horror, I heard sharp intakes of breath as I gave them what were meant to be the heartening statistics before the dispiriting ones (such as that each month, London's hugely successful Kensington Place restaurant serves 10,000 meals, and just four bottles of vintage port). My point was that although port may still be drunk in quantity by shooting parties and pensioners, it is rapidly losing its place in the modern wine drinker's life, cellar, habits and heart - as witness the collapse of vintage port prices in the auction rooms as investors offload this unfashionable commodity, and the availability of vintage port at almost embarrassingly low prices from merchants as on the ball as Oddbins and Farr Vintners.

Most of my friends, I heartlessly told them, love wine and take such advantage of the hugely improved quality of table wine, that they just cannot afford the time or bloodstream capacity for a super-alcoholic drink at the end of a meal. And if today's thirty- and forty-somethings aren't drinking it, who will?

I did go on to outline various ways of galvanising the wine trade and press, to suggest that they try to promote port with food, and to underline the increasingly popularity of the much lighter and more versatile tawny port that, unlike vintage port, needs no decanting and is delicious chilled. But I'm not sure they heard. I suddenly realized that I had probably set back the prospects for women being allowed into the British Association by several millenia. I really did think I was being informative and constructive but I suppose if you are a member of a port shipping family you do drink a lot of port and make sure that your friends do too, so are inevitably somewhat sheltered from the cruel caprices of the marketplace.

You are also, and this is surely the key, much more limited in the quality and range of wines drunk before the port. The only way to savour port is probably to plan ahead for it by deliberate restraint en route.

The way to enjoy vintage port to the full, I suspect, is to stand the heavily sedimented bottles up for a few days before decanting them, invite punctual guests, give them a little interesting rather than stunning wine to begin with, and to make the cheese/sweet/dessert section of a dinner its focal point. I for one owe it to my sisters in Oporto to put this into practice.

December 5, 1992

This article elicited considerable correspondence (perhaps because those with time to write such letters have the time to drink port?) including a handwritten letter from the British Ambassador to France who thought my article "was full of good sense".

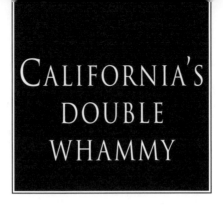

CALIFORNIA'S DOUBLE WHAMMY

B y now nurseryman Rich Kunde of Sonoma Grapevines would normally have grafted more than half a million vines for sale to California's grape growers. This year he hasn't grafted a single one.

This is despite the fact that demand for young vine cuttings in California has never been greater. Thanks to the predations of a new strain of the dreaded plant louse phylloxera, which devastated the vineyards of Europe and beyond a century ago, Californians are engaged in a major vineyard replanting programme. The only known deterrent is to graft vines on to phylloxera-resistant rootstocks. The AxR-1 rootstocks on which the California wine industry has depended have been productive but just not resistant enough.

According to some estimates the majority of vineyards in Napa and Sonoma, California's most famous wine regions, will have to be completely replanted over the next decade, but Mr Kunde (and a handful of others) knows something so serious that, as he puts it, "it could be a tidal wave that will make the phylloxera thing look like a little ripple."

For decades Davis, the world-famous University of California wine research centre, has prided itself as the world's prime source of virus-free vine cuttings from its solid-sounding Foundation Plant Materials Service. Virus diseases have throughout history wreaked almost as much damage as phylloxera on the world's vineyards. Fanleaf is bad but the worst is leafroll virus, probably caused by a group of viruses, which can halve yields but also slows ripening so that the resultant wines are thin and tart.

Leafroll's chief symptom is visible only on some varieties and only during the autumn when leaves of certain red wine vines may turn over on themselves and take on deceptively beautiful autumnal colours. It is particularly difficult to detect because on some varieties, and all rootstocks (which are essential for California's phylloxera-resistant replanting programme), there are no visible symptoms at all.

For years it has been taught, and believed, that leafroll can be spread only by using cuttings from infected plants. But last summer the FPMS at Davis began testing the all-important 'mother vines' for leafroll using the sophisticated ELISA technique developed in the early 1980s, to ensure that the millions of cuttings released to vine growers all over the world each year really are virus-free. The plant pathologist found to his horror that about 20 per cent of some batches tested positive, even though they had been selected from virus-free plants. Aaargh!

The situation progressed from sleepless nights to shared knowledge to task forces to decisions and on December 16 the FPMS issued a letter explaining why they had stopped issuing plant material, admitting that the virus seems to be spreading through their supposedly virus-free Foundation Vineyard and they have not a clue how. This rather elliptical communication, however, may still be languishing at the bottom of various holiday in-trays. The real showdown will take place this Tuesday at a meeting with California nurserymen and grape growers.

They are confused enough already by what they call the latent virus phenomenon, whereby cuttings taken from vines that performed superbly when grafted on to AxR-1 rootstocks, show horrible virus symptoms now that they are being grafted on to phylloxera-resistant rootstocks. Not to mention the nasty Pierce's disease for which there is no known cure and which is a particular problem in southern California and in some Napa vineyards.

Not that leafroll spread has come out of the blue. Some observers had noticed leafroll in the Davis vineyards some time ago, but it was not taken seriously. Leafroll had also appeared in New Zealand's National Foundation Vineyard, made up of cuttings imported from Davis, some years back. But again, it was ignored because everyone believed leafroll could only be spread from infected vines and these were vines guaranteed by Davis to be virus-free. In Taiwan, another FPMS client had noticed strange patterns of virus spread too, as had some growers in Europe and South Africa, it now emerges.

Although no-one knows how the virus is spreading, and a definitive answer within less than a few years seems unlikely, a vector, an insect perhaps, is implicated. Mealy bug is currently the prime suspect.

And leafroll is not only difficult to spot, it is impossible to cure. So Californians who have just replanted a vineyard after pulling it out after the predations of phylloxera now cannot be sure that they have not in fact planted virused vines and/or virused rootstocks which will have to pulled up again when, only after three years or so, they can monitor the vines' performance. International viticulturalist Dr Richard Smart has already advised clients in Australia as well as California to pull out any vines showing signs of leafroll, especially if mealy bug is present - unwelcome advice when vines are expected to produce for up to 30 years but take three years to establish in the vineyard. What a blow to an industry that so recently looked so rosy. For the moment, growers may be paralysed and nurseryman such as Kunde can do little other than hope that it was ELISA at fault all along. Instead of grafting new cuttings for sale, he is currently instituting painstaking tracking systems whereby every cutting among the millions he has sold can be traced right back to its source.

According to Warren Winiarski of Stag's Leap, one of Napa's most viticulturally aware wine producers, "there is now a great deal of uncertainty about how rapidly we can go forward with this replanting program. We may move out of the phylloxera frying pan into the fire of these viruses, Pierce's disease and so on".

Where to gather ye rosebuds? Whatever happens, California's best wines, which (unlike most from the New World) have real distinction and subtlety, are unlikely to get any cheaper. Morris & Verdin of London SE1 (0171-357 8866) import one of the UK's most interesting selections, including Au Bon Climat and Boony Doon's deliberately quirky range. Bibendum of London NW1 (0171-722 5577) and of York (01423 330131) also try harder than most, with Chalk Hill, Saintsbury, and Kistler's divine 1990 McCrea Chardonnay actually worth the premier cru price, £17.50, asked for it. Bonny Doon, Mt Eden, Rochioli Pinot Noir and Joseph Swan Zinfandel are available from Raeburn Fine Wines of Edinburgh (0131-332 5166). Ridge Geyserville Zinfandel is increasingly well distributed (Les Amis du Vin, London W1 and Safeway) while John Armit Wines of London W11 has Ravenswood Zinfandel. Meanwhile, Oddbins are committed to nosing out California bargains.

January 16, 1993

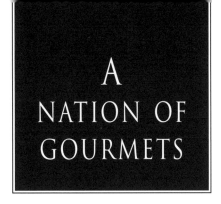

A
NATION OF
GOURMETS

I have become very interested in Belgians recently. The French may take wine and food seriously but they are babes in arms compared with the Belgians. I say this with all the authority of one who spent a whole weekend in Leuwen - or was it Louvain? - last autumn and who spent far too much of a day late last year being interviewed, in London, for a Belgian magazine. It is rare for the interviewee to learn more than the interviewer, but I'm sure I did on this occasion.

The man from Brussels got little out of our encounter, other than exasperation at my inability to get to grips with his dauntingly all-embracing instruction, 'Tell me about European wine'. But he had brought with him a Belgian photographer, a truly fascinating young man who had been brought up in a restaurant, his father being a restaurateur. Thus, although the young Belgian was there in clicker mode, he couldn't help passing on epicureanisms in the restaurant where we met for lunch.

That was my first mistake. I suggested we meet at Clarke's, Sally Clarke's Kensington restaurant with a California accent on both its food and wine. It therefore proved rather more difficult than it might otherwise have been to field the bottles of European wine required for the photograph.

Nor could my two Belgian friends quite believe that the fresh face at the char grill belonged not just to the chef but to the patron. While we waited for our first course, the photographer asked politely where she had trained. I would have liked a photograph of his face when I told him California.

Soon after this the wine arrived. Assuming they would be interested to taste something out of the ordinary, I had ordered a bottle of Au Bon Climat Chardonnay. The name may be French but the provenance is an old barn in California's Santa Barbara County. They viewed it rather as one might a dog with three legs.

But the photographer was particularly worried about the means used to cool the bottle. "I was taught", he said, "that you should never cool wine in a fridge, only in an ice bucket." I can see the logic of this if you are running a restaurant full of faultfinding Belgians. Wines, especially fizzy ones, left for more than a few days in a fridge can lose their fruit, and stock rotation is much more difficult in a restaurant than at home. But my photographer friend clearly thought that wine itself is capable of sensing by which method it is being transformed from temperature A to B, and of reacting accordingly.

"Excuse me", he then asked politely over the first course, "but would you normally drink wine with soup? I was taught you never should." An interesting point that, and one we discussed at some length. We had ordered the wine before choosing our food and I hadn't given it a moment's thought. It is certainly true that since soup slakes thirst, there should be no need to drink anything with it, but I couldn't convince the photographer that there was nothing about the flavour of soup per se that was inherently inimical to wine. In Belgium, however, you do not serve wine with soup. I felt bad about making him party to this solecism.

Then we all started to discuss corkscrews. The Belgians were horrified by my enthusiasm for the Screwpull Lever model (which has transformed my life, involving as it sometimes does the extraction of more than 50 corks a day). But, they pointed out in unison, there is the possibility that the point of the screw might emerge below the cork and push a particle of said cork into the wine. So what? I said. The interviewer scribbled madly. "We've got a right revolutionary here." said his furtive look to the photographer.

All of this instructive observation of assumed national behaviour had been presaged by my Belgian weekend where a group of us wine tasters had our knees under some table almost every waking hour (although we did spend a lot of time snoozing in the back of limos between meals).

Tastings would be punctuated by little plateful of truffle or foie gras, and every glass was religiously rinsed with the relevant wine, even precious Yquem, before being used for tasting (and we must have tasted at least five dozen wines during the weekend). Wine thermometers were much in evidence. Our host's son had driven 800 kilometers (500 miles) to Epernay to buy the right sort of beef for Sunday lunch. Whenever a course was served it was fallen upon and ravished in a noisy though wordless food-dedicated interval before the upright position and conversation could be resumed.

But the most riveting sight, the one that convinced me that a Belgian's vocation is to eat and drink, was of a piece of gastronomic equipment which I have never encountered elsewhere but which raised not an eyebrow in Belgian company. Just before each meal the really keen members of our party would take from their pockets or handbags a small chain about a foot long with an ornamental clip at each end and reverently arrange them round the back of the neck before using them to clip their napkins neatly up to the chin.

The ritual unclipping was invariably accompanied by a sigh of sated melancholy.

For a thoroughly Belgian antidote to all this reverence, Londoners should head for the impressively, jokily, spartan Belgo restaurant in Chalk Farm Road, NW1 [or the more recent Belgo Central in Covent Garden, WC2]. Great value for moules and beers to turn the head of the most convinced wine lover.

February 20, 1993

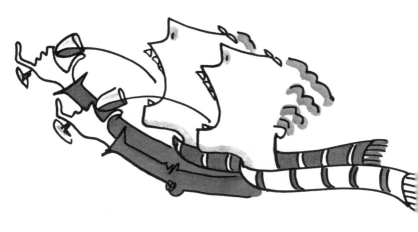

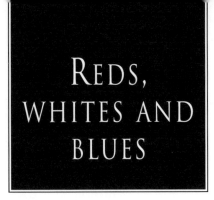

REDS, WHITES AND BLUES

Oxbridge rivalry is supposed to run deepest in the river Thames between Putney and Mortlake, isn't it? But this year's Boat Race can hardly be more acrimonious than the Oxford v. Cambridge Wine Tasting Match held in London earlier this month.

This, the 40th annual such blind tasting, had all the usual hallmarks of varsity confrontation: Cambridge accusing Oxford of weighting the boat with too many graduates; women playing the most minor of roles; and certain amount of exhibitionism. The cocktail was headily spiked, however, with a few distinctly nineties ingredients: gratuitious legal wrangling, the strong whiff of hard-edged commercialism, and calculated yobbishness.

The Cambridge captain, a third year lawyer currently choosing between four investment banks' offers of employment, was proud of the contract he'd spent "hundreds of pounds' worth of faxes and paper" drawing up between his team and the competition's sponsors Pol Roger champagne. "We're the first team to realise the commercial value of all this," he said proudly, nodding at his fellow competitors slurping Pol Roger wines round the celebratory lunch table at London's Oxford & Cambridge Club.

"Yeah," said his vice captain, an American who declared, not entirely coherently, he could be as rude as he liked since next week he'd be at Yale, "teaching scumbags European History". This charming fellow, just two seats away from the organiser of the event, the mildmannered Master of Wine who represents Pol Roger in England, noisily (and erroneously) laid into the quality of the champagne being hosed into our glasses. He boasted that they, Cambridge, had talked about offering the sponsorship deal to their preferred champagne Bollinger, and it was only by agreeing to the lawyer captain's strict terms and conditions that Pol Roger had secured the privilege of laying on this competition and lunch.

With an eye to relatively extensive press coverage last year (helped enormously by *New York Times* wine writer Frank Prial's entirely flukey presence in London SW1 that day), the Cambridge captain had tried to polish up the participants' image. "We didn't want to look like a lot of rich layabouts, so I made Pol Roger change the prize to a cheque for £1,000 to a charity chosen by the winners."

No, he hadn't actually thought about which their charity would be, which was perhaps just as well since Cambridge lost, by 744 points to 855 (out of a possible 1,440), despite fielding one young Australian who dropped only 12 points out of a maximum of 120 points in the white wine 'paper'. The captain/business manager had clearly put more energy into the subclauses than into coaching his team. Younger Cambridge tasters talked wistfully of how much they could have learnt by tasting together and sharing impressions before the big day, a process assiduously encouraged at Oxford.

While Cambridge fielded the regulation stubble wearer with FT folded ostentatiously into a Samuel Beckett paperback, Oxford's team was long on neatly dressed mathematicians and democracy (joint captains and a positive bias in favour of women, even if only two of their final eight were female in the end). The opposing captains nearly came to blows across the table when the question of graduate participation was broached. "But our graduates are relatively inexperienced tasters", was Oxford's defence of the maturity of its team.

Oh and the wines themselves? Forgive me, they seemed rather peripheral to the event. A New Zealand Sauvignon Blanc (1991 from Selaks) was spotted by almost everyone, even the judges myself and Hugh Johnson, along with a full throttle Australian Chardonnay (1990 from Tim Knappstein) and a mature rioja, Viña Ardanza Reserva 1985. Best wines there were probably Ch Léoville Las-Cases 1985 (Cambridge had contracted Pol Roger to lay on some smart wines) and Mascarello's Barbaresco Marcarini 1985 (£17.99 from Winecellars of London SW18). The worst wine by far was an unexpectedly oxidized Meursault, Narvaux 1989 from Boyer-Martinot, which some of the participants loved. This did not surprise me one little bit.

March 6, 1993

GETTING TO GRIPS WITH THE R WORD

Wine names are full of pronunciation traps. Cos, Montrachet and Moët can all sort out the Moutons from the goats, but the most commonly mispronounced name of all must be Riesling, which is 'Reece-ling' and not 'Rise-ling'. This is all the more lamentable since Riesling is the greatest white wine grape of all, lives for ever and, as demonstrated eloquently at recent tastings held in Paris, London and New York, does not have to be sweet to be good.

The tastings could not be concurrent since they were the child of one brain, whose owner was understandably keen to attend each one. Stuart Pigott is a dedicatedly non-partisan wine writer in his early thirties who sees his mission as sniffing out some of the finest wines being made today, wherever they may be.

His particular speciality is Riesling, about which he has written four books (two of them self-published guides to the best wines made in Germany in 1989 and 1990), and he has for years wanted to set up a blind comparison of the finest Rieslings of the world.

The super-concentrated 1990 vintage at last provided him with an even playing field for the Rieslings of Germany, Austria and Alsace in France. And he had to choose the razor-sharp dry style of Riesling since that is just about all Alsace produces. Germany and Austria used to make predominantly sweet wines, and British and American wine merchants still import little else, but within both Austria and Germany there has been a winemaking revolution, partly provoked by the 1985 diethylene glycol scandal in which only sweet wines were implicated.

Thus, since about 1988, almost all regions of Germany and, in particular, the cool and dramatic Wachau district of Austria make a wide range of fully fermented, non-sweetened Rieslings in the racy style of Alsace (which style has in any case been the only acceptable form of Riesling for many younger British and American wine drinkers). The Pigott tasting, held at the Gavroche with Riedel glasses as indications of seriousness of intent, comprised six flights of wines (this collective noun for once seeming appropriate, given the airborne quality of fine dry Rieslings) of which a dozen came from each of Austria and Germany and 10 from Alsace.

"This tasting is in many ways the most impossible thing I've ever tried to do, because of the impossible combination of political interests" was his somewhat devigorated comment on the machinations involved in persuading the three generic promotional bodies concerned to underwrite such a potentially damaging exercise. In the event, what was extraordinary to me was the similarity in style between the wines, yet the dissimilarity between that style and the stereotypical descriptions of Riesling. There was hardly a wine that could be described as 'flowery', while Riesling, like any great grape variety, proved itself as a vehicle for transmitting location.

Virtually all of the producers seemed to be trying to pack as much concentration and local character into the bottle as possible, so that many were marked much more by a distinctly mineral note, with explosive, but definitely dry fruit on the palate. Lime, wet stones, gunsmoke, paprika, honey and even salami cropped up in my tasting notes, and they were all beautifully balanced, except for some very ripe wines in which the alcohol was just a bit too much for this delicately transparent grape variety.

As has become customary at any serious blind comparative tasting (especially one funded by the participants), we were urged at the beginning that this was Not A Competition. But, as has also become customary, there was a show of hands for favourite wines at the end. The London favourite seemed to be an Austrian, a Dürnsteiner Kellerberg Smaragd from the Wachau magician F X Pichler, which had been second favourite in Paris where, perhaps not surprisingly, an Alsace wine had been favoured, Marcel Deiss's Schoenenburg (£22.50 from Lea & Sandeman, see below).

It is difficult to exaggerate how well a top quality dry Riesling goes with food - far better than most Chardonnays which can be extremely blunt instruments to apply to the palate and head at the start of a meal. High acid plus relatively low alcohol, now minus sugar, should equal success for this exciting new style of fine wine.

Where to buy dry Rieslings: It is near impossible to find the lovely Wachau Rieslings outside Austria, and the dry Rieslings so treasured by Germans are only slowly escaping that country (although try Philip Eyres of Amersham on 01494 433823, Gelston Castle in

Scotland on 01556 3012, Oddbins and Summerlee Wines of Earls
Barton on 01604 810488 for names such as Juliusspital, Koehler
Ruprecht, Lingenfelder, Müller Catoir,). Unpatriated top quality dry
Alsace Riesling is much easier to find. Adnams of Southwold on
01502 724222 sell Blanck wines; Lea & Sandeman of London SW10
and W8 on 0171-376 4767 have Deiss; O W Loeb of London SE1 on
0171-928 7750 have Faller, and Hugel; Morris & Verdin of SW1 on
0171-630 888 have Ostertag; Thresher/Wine Rack/Bottoms Up have
Zind-Humbrecht; and La Vigneronne of London SW7 on 0171-589
6113 has a wide range of Alsace including Kreydenweiss.

March 20, 1993

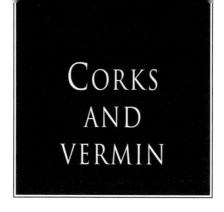

CORKS
AND
VERMIN

"What you are going to see will strike you as primitive. 'Isn't there another way?' you will wonder. Yes there is, and it will eventually be implemented." This was how the export director of the world's biggest cork company prepared me for the second half of a tour that had not, even up to that point, been distinguished by sophistication.

Amorim & Irmão's cork processing plant just south of Oporto is a tenebrous hangar the size of 16 football pitches. Hanging in the dark rafters is the sweet smell of boiling cork bark for, before anything else happens to it, each man-sized strip of bark is boiled for 90 minutes in ancient, blackened cauldrons to soften it and, it is hoped, eliminate the harsh elements and any taints.

On the rough earth floor are steaming piles of cork bark, covered with patches that can look alarmingly like mould. After drying, these coarse strips of bark are then picked over by keen-eyed factory workers, graded, and neatened up (just as they were a century ago) in preparation for the next stage in the process, the manual, popgun punching of corks from strips of bark which Antonio Affonso de Barros is so anxious to modernise. All it will take is a bank of laser scanners and an awful lot of Escudos.

The wine cork business is in turmoil, and it has nothing to do with how corks are punched. The wine world is kicking up a stink about the unreliability of its traditional stopper. Modernists object to grappling with a corkscrew and a bit of bark. Everyone, some of them muttering about cork trees being stripped too young, feels that the incidence of 'corked' bottles - containing wine rendered undrinkably smelly, presumably by a tainted cork - is too high.

Some reports put the incidence at one in 12, which is surely an exaggeration. No more than one in every 50 to 100 bottles I open shows any corked character, although I have noticed an increase in the incidence of cork policemen, as in "this wine's a bit corked, isn't it?" And once the suggestion is made, it is difficult to resist, especially if resistance implies that your nose is less sensitive than the cork policeman's.

Research has isolated the chief suspect, a substance called TCA for short, which results from an unhealthy blend of chlorine, moisture, mould and phenols and turns a wine's aroma into an odour. It has also been found in uncorked liquids, however, presumably as a result of chlorinated water and less-than-clean storage containers, thus providing the cork manufacturers with a little defensive ammunition. "We are fully aware that the cork is a very unwelcome element in the wine package," Sr Affonso de Barros told me wearily, "but look at the alternatives. Is there really anything that can be made by machine, offers a reliable seal, is inert to wine and is also easily extractable?"

Top contender on all these counts is the humble crown cap, the one that has to be levered off beer bottles, so humble I am not even sure how it is known in the closures trade. It is also considerably cheaper than cork and fails principally on aesthetic grounds, probably because, I would suggest, the yanked elbow is an action so much less elegant than the sommelier's current graceful arc.

The screwcap has the advantage of being resealable, but cannot offer a perfect seal in the first place if temperatures rise. And the plastic cork substitute surely combines the worst of all worlds, except that it should be much easier to keep free of TCA.

The cork industry itself has been slowly wielding a new broom to push TCA out of their antiquated warehouses. Most producers offer hydrogen peroxide treatments in place of the old chlorine bleaching which, as monitored by David Ramey of Chalk Hill, one of California's most scientifically rigorous winemakers, has virtually eliminated the problem of 'corkiness' now that cork producers have reduced the amount of hydrogen peroxide used.

Cork producers continue to offer both chlorine bleached and hydrogen peroxide-treated corks, however, and according to Sr Affonso de Barros, many of the cork brokers on whom the wine trade depends have been slow to accept the new, chlorine-free model. Amorim are also perfecting a special non-chemical heat treatment, although so far this is available only for champagne sorry, sparkling wine - corks.

I have long argued that the gap between the cork trade and the wine trade was unnecessarily wide, and too wide to permit vital communication between the two. Affonso de Barros did actually spend eight "fascinating" years of his working life working for the other side, as a director of purchasing for the huge Seagram organisation in Oporto and thus as a major buyer, rather than seller, of corks.

He claims - but then he would, wouldn't he - that much of the problem lies in wine producers' treatment of corks. They tend to be shipped around the world in large plastic bags which should be stored within fairly narrow ranges of temperature and humidity. He's seen them stored just under a hot tin roof in Australia, for example, and would like to see cork cosseting included in the syllabus of all wine-making courses. "Many of these problems could be avoided if the wine industry were willing to co-operate in depth with the cork industry by exchanging views and taking advice."

During current hostilities, this seems all too unlikely. But is the wine trade really prepared for life without a pop?

April 10, 1993

I thought this an unusually even-handed article on a contentious subject. Mr Affonso de Barros, unfortunately, did not and faxed his comments which ended "You are not to be congratulated on this one and I am sure we will be exposed to some more of your verminous prose."

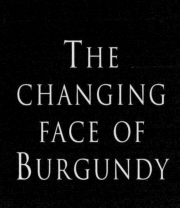

THE CHANGING FACE OF BURGUNDY

Thirty-one year-old Jean-Philippe Fichet is typical of a new breed of Burgundian. He was brought up in the village of Meursault, a name that spells gold, glory, and expense, to white wine lovers. Like most of his contemporaries, he comes from a family of vignerons. His father has 5.5 ha (14 acres) of vines in Meursault and the neighbouring villages of Chassagne-Montrachet and Puligny-Montrachet. Like most of the older generation, Fichet Père has always sold his wine in bulk to the negociants, the big wine merchants of Beaune.

Thus the name Fichet is not known to the wide wine-buying public, only to the brokers or courtiers who have until recently trawled the region for wine to pour into the negociant blends carrying the famous village and vineyard names of Burgundy. Until very recently Fichet was a name on sample bottles rather than wine labels.

But Jean-Philippe realised, or perhaps sensed more intuitively, his roots being so deep in the poor soils of Burgundy, that his father's way would not be his way forward towards the next millenium of Burgundian history. He wants, quite simply, to make great wine, and to see it enjoyed with his own name on it.

He has seen what his cousin Jean-François Coche-Dury has achieved by establishing his Domaine. By doing everything possible to maximise quality at the expense of quantity, Coche-Dury can sell every bottle he makes three times over. And yet he still sells the less successful wine he makes in bulk to the negociants. Such dedication can hardly fail to inspire.

Young Fichet's motivation is far from financial. He is heavily in debt and reckons it will be at least 10 years before Domaine

Jean-Philippe Fichet does anything more than cover its costs, but his ambition makes even more sense now that the negociants' warehouses are full and their prices have tumbled. (In 1989 they were paying 5,000 francs for a barrel of Bourgogne Blanc and 15,000 francs for Meursault; today they will pay only 1,000 and 6,000 respectively.)

He has been making wine for 11 years now, since he was 20, but happily admits that it has been only for the last four years, from the 1989 vintage, that he has been making good wine (although even his 1987 and 1988 vintages were praised in the influential American Robert Parker's book 'Burgundy').

Jean-Philippe, who exports 60 per cent of his small production, realises he needs to expand his horizons outside the village of Meursault. He accordingly made his first trip to England last month to show his wines at the annual Burgundy tasting of his UK importers Morris & Verdin. Jasper Morris delightedly told him about a blind tasting championship held recently for Winecellars customers in London to assess the relative merits of France, Italy and Australia at various price levels. It was apparently entirely due to the almost unanimous enthusiasm for Jean-Philippe Fichet's Bourgogne Rouge 1990 (£68 a case from Morris & Verdin) that France 'won' overall, but the young Frenchman was unimpressed. "Wait till you see my 1992", he said with a smile.

Fichet admits that he is a terrible taster, in the sense that, like any passionate winemaker, no matter what the wine, he is always looking for its faults. He says he has learnt by hanging around those whose wines he admires, such as cousin Coche, François Jobard and Dominique Lafon of Meursault's famous Domaine Comte Lafon ("although someone like Dominique isn't going to tell me all his secrets", he says admiringly).

Although his passionate dedication to quality is shared by an increasing number of young vignerons all over Europe, people who a generation ago might have left the countryside rather than inherit an agricultural way of life, surely many of his contemporaries are just coasting along on the endangered reputation of yesterday's Burgundy? Isn't it difficult to maintain friendships when at such professional variance? Strange that the French don't have a word for the shrug they employ so usefully.

Dissatisfied with the temperature and humidity in his initial rented cave, he set about finding the sort of "silent, secret place" he thinks great wine needs. He is now renting a deeper, larger cellar from the Commune of Meursault where he can boast of a fairly constant, natural 16 C and nice, damp conditions to keep the oak barrels supple. He is wary of new wood and uses it sparingly only for his very best wines, but understands the importance of establishing a rapport with his cooper, Damy in Meursault. "You can't just ring up 10 days before harvest and expect to get the best barrels", he says.

In little plots around Meursault, Chassagne, Monthélie and Volnay, Fichet now owns just 2 ha (5 acres) of red and white vines and is renting a further 5 ha (12.5 acres) as a sharecropper, which means he cannot reduce yields as much as he would like. When his father retires, his three siblings will leave him free to take over the family vines and practise the ultra-strict pruning he believes necessary to squeeze extra concentration into the resulting wines.

But what does his father think of his son's, quite different working philosophy? "Ah," smiles Jean-Philippe ruefully. "It is the job of a father not to say anything. But what I think he thinks is that what I am doing is sensible for today's conditions."

Fichet wines, of which the mealy Meursault 1990 is a star, are available from Morris & Verdin, London SE1 (0171 357 8866). Coche Dury wines are (sometimes) available from Lay & Wheeler of Colchester (01206 764446) and Winecellars are based in Wandsworth, London SW18 (0181-871 2668).

May 1, 1993

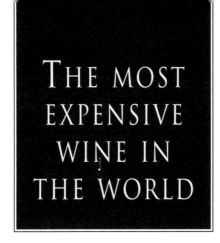

THE MOST EXPENSIVE WINE IN THE WORLD

I n my nearly 20 years as a wine groupie I have been to many seriously grand tastings. An over-comprehensive look at the 1959 claret vintage springs to mind. Much more clearly than any single wine, I remember an Irishman whispering as we filed solemnly into a chamber full of tasting samples, "If only we could actually drink *one* of these wines with dinner tonight".

At least I remember the glory of the Ch Latour à Pomerol among the vast 1961 tasting I played hookey from the launch of my own television series to attend. Claret is the most common tasting subject because it is a long-lived wine produced in quantity, and submits neatly to being divided 'horizontally' (same vintage, different châteaux) or 'vertically' (same château, different vintages). My tasting file is stuffed with the purple-spotted notes on such events.

But it was not until last April that I came across a tasting of the world's most expensive claret, Ch Pétrus, £800 a dozen bottles in a dire vintage; several thousand in a good one. Perhaps this is partly because the British, so few of whom can afford it, tend to look very, very slightly down their noses at it. It is Pomerol, for a start, a parvenu that affords dangerously instant gratification. No pain is associated with tasting fleshy young Pomerol, which does not suit the masochist brigade reared on tannic young Pauillac and St Estèphe.

For this reason London is not the most likely place for a Pétrus tasting - but I hardly expected to come across one in the backwoods of rural France. In fact, seasoned observers like me do not expect to come across consumer wine tastings of any sort anywhere in France outside the capital. Wine tasting is not the leisure activity in France it has become for British consumers.

But here it was, lying in the reception of a smartish hotel in the depths of the French countryside, where the average annual income must be well under 100,000 FF, an application form for tickets, at 1850FF, for a forthcoming tasting of Pétrus. Seven vintages back to 1945, if you please. And the very night before I was due to leave.

The organiser of this unmissable event, tied in to an auction also held at the hotel which I still kick myself for missing, is Michel Fauveau, who works on Toulouse's huge aerospatial campus. (When I asked him what he did, he told me, "I observe the Earth".) An obvious obsessive, he has transformed his obsession with wine into the Club Oenophile du Midi (tel 61.27.37.69 or 62.24.43.34).

The organisation of the event was fascinatingly different from the British norm. For a start, the application form included the question 'Are you familiar with wine tasting?' which I cannot imagine being asked in Britain. Nor can I imagine M. Fauveau's British counterpart demanding verbal input, as in the classroom, from tasters who had paid more than £200 for the experience.

And I would not have thought many Brits would have dared, like the auctioneer, to stroll into the tasting room with a cigar. Yet the average age of the 28 assembled tasters (for two bottles of each vintage, a generous serving) was impressively low, partly reduced by a member of the French national football team and his entourage.

As it would probably be wherever it was held, the tasting was presented by a noted expert, in this case the Pétrus winemaker Jean-Claude Berrouet himself who shares with his employer Christian Moueix a sensible view of wine's place in life. He pointed out somewhat ruefully that wine tasting per se is something new in France, something '*très Anglo-Saxon*'. The point of wine, he quite rightly stressed, is to be drunk, preferably at a table with food.

And that was another important national distinguishing mark. You can spend a lifetime at wine tastings in Britain before anyone mentions food, but at this early evening tasting M. Berrouet and most other commentators suggested dishes, increasingly specific dishes as dinnertime approached, to go with each wine. With the 1945, in decline and smelling of 'a nice eighteenth century *manoir*', a tableful of local doctors proposed *ris de veau aux truffes*.

It was hard to discern any national variation in taste, but since no activity is more subjective than wine tasting, this is hardly surprising. There were considerable variations between the bottles in the older vintages, but the 1966 that reached the table I shared with Madame Fauveau was a dream: seductive, tannin-free, headily perfumed, satin textured and much more concentrated than our bottle of the often vaunted 1967.

I was also bowled over by the 1982 which is intense and meaty and has many years to go, and the 1962 (made, as M. Berrouet was careful to point out, when there wasn't a single oenologist, or qualified winemaker, in the Pomerol region) was also fabulous, tasting provocatively close to its peak. The rich, almost porty 1971 with its notes of chocolate and coffee is another vintage the seriously rich should be thinking of clearing out of their cellars, while the 1975 was a delightful surprise, the vintage's notorious tannins well in retreat.

For me, this had been a truly sensational tasting, breaking new ground in both subject and location, but I had to wait just 48 hours before being put in my place. At a double magnum dinner back in London, admittedly designed for seriously rich wine collectors, I met a Belgian who told me that at his Pétrus tasting he had not only had all the vintages, but all seven bottlings of the ne plus ultra 1947 vintage. I wonder if he's happier than I am?

May 29, 1993

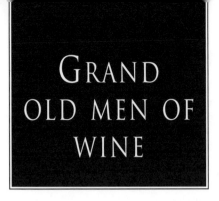

GRAND OLD MEN OF WINE

The two grandest, oldest men of wine prove that drinking fine wine may make you live longer, but is unlikely to make you rich. Harry Waugh, born 1904, was one of the mould-breaking British wine merchants of the 1950s and 1960s. He helped introduce a little-known wine called Pétrus to Britain, encouraged the entirely new phenomenon of domaine bottling in Burgundy, and was singing the praises of California wine about a decade before anyone else outside the state did so.

He left Harveys of Bristol in 1966 when it was bought by Showerings, of Babycham fame, but retained his directorship of the Bordeaux first growth Château Latour and a pension which did not take account of either inflation or the fact that he was to become a father, of twins, seven years later.

At Harveys he trained many of the most famously successful men in today's wine trade, including, ironically enough, the chairman of Allied-Lyons which has just sold Latour back into French, determinedly French, hands, thereby leaving the wine trade's most respected figure, a hale, straight-backed 89 year-old, in urgent need of a financial manager.

Born in Moscow, three years earlier than Harry Waugh in 1901, André Tchelistcheff is an even more remarkable fellow. After surviving severe illness in childhood, and a particularly bloody campaign in the White Russian army in his teens, he trained in agriculture in Czechoslovakia and Paris and specialised in wine only at the age of 36, when he was recruited to impart 'Frenchness', including the technical probity of Pasteur, to Beaulieu Vineyards in California. He could have gone to China instead, like his best friend who became Mao's Minister of Agriculture.

Instead, this intelligent scientist-philosopher has come to be regarded as the father of modern California wine. He pioneered cool fermentation, controlling malolactic fermentation, developed the anti-frost damage wind machines that are such a visible feature of the Napa Valley to this day, and has been consultant at scores of wineries both in America and Europe.

At 92 he has just completed a six week tour of European wine-making friends and vineyards which he describes as 'education'. This was supposed to be his last trip to Europe, but his wife Dorothy over-heard him volunteering at Burgundy's Domaine de la Romanée-Conti to take up an apprenticeship next year.

Only someone with near divine knowledge would claim such ignorance. With the look (including hairstyle) and stature of an imp-ish prep school boy, André Tchelistcheff 's understanding of the wine world is still devastatingly acute, well-informed, and often unexpect-ed. In a soft, still heavily accented voice, he presents perhaps the only analysis of the wine world that has ever been based on such a long history and such a wide geographical purview.

Acknowledging the demands of the technically curious but impatient modern wine consumer, he observes, for example, that 'wines are naked at the moment. And this is a good thing because it is good to show one's deficiences. Little by little winemakers will learn what the consumer wants of his wines and will begin to reclothe them. Pumping over the grape must is the key.' André Tchelistcheff believes that wines will never again be designed expressly for long ageing in bottle.

He is also blunt about the phylloxera vine pest currently destroying a good part of the northern California vineyard: 'it's the grape growers' fault. They chose to plant a rootstock they knew did not have good phylloxera resistance'.

His palate is as keen as ever, although he drinks sparingly, spar-ing his frail knees in particular. He must have been one of the few visitors to have done a three day stint at this year's Vinexpo, Bordeaux's notoriously exhausting international wine exhibition, and certainly the only nonogenarian to walk the full length of the exhibi-tion hall. Dorothy, whose arm enabled the feat, heard many a hissed 'that's André Tchelistcheff' as they made their progress, presumably from one grandson of an old associate to the next.

One of the consultancies which has thrilled him most has been with Château Ste Michelle, the giant of Washington state, where he believes there may be greater potential than California. He is still quoted, admired, and decorated amid much ballyhoo when it suits the decorators (although as far as he is concerned, it is presumably diffi-cult to better the Chevalier du Mérite Agricole awarded by the

French as early as 1954 for his part in Frenchifying the American wine industry).

Considering his input to the world's ritziest wine industry, André Tchelistcheff lives modestly, has never had a wine cellar of his own, and seems to have encountered more difficulties during his six week tour of Europe than one would think fit for an eminent 94 year-old. One major blow was a letter from Lodovico Antinori of Ornellaia in Tuscany maintaining that he could no longer afford the services of the consultant whose name appears in so much of his promotional literature.

And then there was the fact that they spent their first night in Britain last month in the just opened Ibis hotel at Heathrow. We should have organised a troika with outriders and given them, and Harry Waugh and his wife, the run of the grand new Vintners' Place development overlooking the Thames.

September 11, 1993

André Tchelistcheff never did serve his DRC apprenticeship. He died in spring 1994.

W hen I first spoke on the telephone to Geoff Merrill, South Australian winemaker extraordinaire, he was still recovering from Ian Botham's most recent testimonial. He had got to bed at quarter to four in the morning and had to be on a 7.55 flight to Rome. He made it. He kept his promise to Sainsbury's to go and see some Orvieto and Frascati fermentations bubbling away before turning his hired Lancia north and driving 680 km to position himself in readiness for a hard day's winemaking the next day.

'I've been told I must have been the most photographed person in Italy last September, the speeds I been doing on those autostradas', he told me when I met him on his next visit to London. 'Excuse the verbal diarrohea. Had m'fortieth last night. Went upstairs to brush m'teeth at four o'clock this morning. Never did get down to help the wife with the clearing up. Beefy Botham didn't even turn up till 11.'

Geoff Merrill is one of those characters whose reputations precede them. Somehow, our paths had never crossed - a lack of cricketing expertise on my part, perhaps - and I was all prepared for Les Paterson incarnate. What I wasn't prepared for on my doorstep was the flowery waistcoated, silk shirted charmer with a bunch of irises and a heavily fertilised handlebar moustache.

Sainsburys's, the most sober of British supermarket chains, has hired Merrill to inject a bit of Australian 'fruit-driven' character into an array of Italian wines made at premises owned by Gruppo Italiano Vini, Italy's most dynamic group of cooperatives. According to eye witnesses, the facial expressions above the Italians' Milanese suits when Merrill was presented to them were worthy of note.

What Merrill didn't realise when he took on the job, the way Australians don't when looking at maps of Europe, is quite how long he would spend in the Lancia between what turned out to be seven different wineries from Rome to the alps.

In one 24 hour stretch he drove 1,600 km. 'I had to work even harder in Italy than I do back home. See everything's in place at Mount Hurtle. You just ring up Coonawarra, say, and get answers to "What's the sugar level? Any sulphide on the nose?"' You can't in Italy. You have to jump in your car in Trento and drive to bloody Rome and back.'

But Merrill swears he loves the Italians. Great people. Great food. Some great wines, especially Tuscan reds. 'The elegant tannins in those Antinori wines. That's what I'm trying to go for at home. I'm not a big rap for Valpolicella, mind you, but I liked those, whaddya-call them, Amarones. That's all I drank up there (in Valpolicella country). Fifteen per cent alcohol, mind you. Not very clever, was it?

'The only thing is, the way those guys eat lunch. You can forget asking someone to give you a reading at five to bloody twelve. Or put some Chardonnay into oak on a Saturday even if it's really ready for it. Could be the start of the shooting season, or something really important like that. And d'you know what? At six o'clock, they go home! Chief winemaker came up to me at the end and shook my hand. "You work very hard", he said. Well I wouldn't want it any other way, quite frankly.'

Merrill's principal amendments to the Italian winemaking recipe were to ferment cooler, and use different yeasts, all the time trying desperately to protect the embryonic wine from oxygen, the obverse of Italian philosophy. 'In terms of machinery, Italians have got it all, but what they don't have is enough refrigeration, and it can be bloody hot out there.'

Whatever Sainsbury's have paid Merrill for his motorway dashes, they seem to have squeezed a reasonable yield from him, with a potential eight different wines from such lacklustre appellations as Frascati given a fashionably Aussie spin, which was presumably Sainsbury's intention.

Merrill claims he took on the job to keep sweet a very important British customer for his own Mount Hurtle Australian wines. Sainsbury's on the other hand realised that only someone who was his own boss would be allowed out.

This is not the first time that a 'flying winemaker' has flown in to an Italian winery during the quiet winemaking season down under. The ubiquitous Jacques Lurton turned out some Basilicata wines last year, and Ricasoli of Tuscany had a little help from South Australia. This year Gaetane Carron, ex Rosemount (Australia), Trimbach

(Alsace) and now at Concha y Toro (Chile), has also been working the vintage all over northern Italy.

Sainsbury's wine buyers are flying out to Verona on Monday to choose from the Merrill/GIV Bianco di Custoza, Pinot Grigio, a couple of Chardonnays, a Veneto Sauvignon, a Cabernet or two, a Teroldego, a Frascati, an Orvieto and trials of varietal Grechetto and Verdello, two of Italy's less exposed grape varieties.

Deciding how to market them may be even more difficult, however. A Vino Merrillo label? The Ozitalia range? Or GIVusabeer?

October 30, 1993

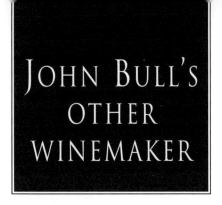

JOHN BULL'S OTHER WINEMAKER

'England is the least advanced place I've ever been to'. This is the sort of thing that gets John Worontschak into trouble with his fellow English winemakers. And how about this extract from an article he wrote in last month's *Which? Wine Monthly* about his introduction to English wine:

'On arrival in 1988, I tasted many bottles of weird-sounding wine - Reichensteiner, Schönburger, etc - all of which purported to have captured that delicate and crisp nature that only England's gentle summers can provide. What I had in my glass was generally thin, over-acidic, oxidised, phenolic and reeking of hydrogen sulphide. My lecturers at wine college used to doctor down wines to this standard and mark the bottles "FOR TEACHING PURPOSES ONLY. DO NOT DRINK."'

Worontschak's fax machine at Twyford in Berkshire has since been buzzing with incoming invective addressed to 'Arrogant Aussie' and worse. He swears there are English wine producers he admires. Three Choirs in Gloucestershire, for instance. But what must be all the more infuriating for Britain's domestic wine industry is that Worontschak's English wines are so damned good, breezily picking up a disproportionate number of accolades and awards.

They have done so by ignoring the German recipe used by most English winemakers, and making dry, fruity, reasonably full bodied, sometimes oaked, rarely aromatic wines, applying theory learnt at Wagga Wagga in torrid New South Wales of all places, to England's quintessentially cool climate, in which grapes have to struggle to ripen at all.

This year with its lack of warmth and surfeit of rain should certainly test Worontschak, with the worst vintage he has seen since arriving at Thames Valley Vineyards in 1988. In his late 20s, having worked 17 vintages in three continents as a cellar rat, progressing towards consultant oenologist, he had despaired of finding the right wine job in France and was working in tele sales in London.

Out of the blue he rang a much older Wagga graduate, in viti-culture, Jon Leighton, knowing vaguely that he had returned to the English Home Counties where he'd spent his youth. Leighton finds himself with 28 acres of Berkshire vineyard because 'for some reason I went to the English Wine Festival in 1978 and haven't been quite the same since'.

Leighton is a first class empirical vine grower, forever refining his trellis systems and pruning regimes, but was in serious need of help in the winery. *Ecco* Worontschak. By the 1989 vintage, many thou-sands of pounds had been spent on the sort of *batterie de cave* that a modern Australian winemaker demands: the gentlest of air bag press-es carefully shielded from oxygen; a £10,000 crusher that filters out the astringent stalks which Worontschak thinks mar so many other English wines; the filter that allows them the luxury of using only free run juice in their own bottlings and transforms the pressings into usable raw material.

But one small winery in some old Berkshire farm buildings was unlikely to hold Worontschak (ex Penfolds, ex Mondavi, ex Beaune) for long. Thus was born the Harvest Wine Group, an association of about 10 vineyards all over southern England for which Worontschak helps make the wine, either at Twyford or on the spot. A recent visit during vintage was punctuated by telephone messages for Worontschak such as 'He's got the grapes sitting in the press, but he doesn't know what setting he should have it on.'

The full Harvest Wine Group range (of about half a million bottles in a good year) is sold by a third colleague based in another spartan outhouse at Thames Valley Vineyards. Maurice Moore also displays a degree of professionalism that is rare in the renascent but still miniature English wine business. The entire range is on sale here at ex cellar, or 'farmgate', prices. But he can also talk major multiples with the best of them and has negotiated own label English wines chez Tesco and Safeway for under £4 a bottle. The focus of the Group, however, is on making money out of English wine by selling serious quality at serious prices, rather than bottled souvenirs on the tourist trail.

A new round of spending has therefore been embarked upon, on the champagne-making equivalent of one of those John Bull DIY printing kits sold in the 1950s and 1960s: a lone automatic riddling pallet, mini disgorger etc. The long term aim is to transform more than half the Twyford grapes into bottle fermented sparkling wine.

This takes advantage of their innate high acidity and neutral flavours, while adding value (for which read price). They claim that their top of the line fizz Leightons, made from Champagne grapes to be released next year at about £13, has been taken for Bollinger by some Champenois.

Good on them. I have tasted only their lesser sparkling blend of English grapes, Ascot at around £9.99, and was less impressed by it than by HWG's admirable range of still wines, which I have served with pride to a number of visiting luminaries from around the wine world.

Worontschak has hired by Tesco to make 1993 wine on their behalf in the Czech Republic (where his family's native Ukrainian can be useful) and will probably be working for them in Cyprus, South Africa, and possibly even Tasmania, next year. Coals to Newcastle, surely?

All wines are available from the Harvest Wine Group, Clocktower Mews, Stanlake Park, Twyford, Berks. 01734 344290 or fax 01734 320914.

November 14, 1993

serve chilled

'The person I abhor most in this world is the professional wine snob. The person I abhor second is the amateur wine snob. And the most boring conversation you can overhear is the two talking together.' The man who used to begin his wine classes thus is one of the few whose assessment of an individual wine I would accept without question.

Almost all of us concerned with selling or advising on wine pay lip service to the notion that the only thing that matters about wine is how it tastes and whether you like it, but no-one has put this maxim into practice as enthusiastically as James Rogers. As a wine merchant and, later, educator and consultant, he has made decisions about individual wines purely on the basis of lining them all up and tasting them without knowing what they were or how much they cost.

'It was my father who told me always to taste blind. "You'll make a fool of ourself for the rest of your life," he said, "but you'll know more than the next person". Wine has certainly taught me honesty and humility.'

A typical Rogers exercise was a lunch last year at which dozens of Britain's more respected palates were invited to taste seven whites and seven reds and put them in order of price. My favourite white, for example, was Umani Ronchi's CaSal di Serra Verdicchio (about £6 at bigger branches of Sainsbury's and Victoria Wine) which I guessed was far more expensive than a perfectly respectable premier cru Chablis. I had never realised how good it was until I had tasted it unsaddled with preconceptions about Verdicchio.

James Rogers could not have come from a more traditional background, and should by rights have become an affable but dozy pinstriped wine merchant. Raised in the leafy lanes of Surrey, he joined Cullens, his family's firm of licensed grocers, as a young failed accountant in 1971. The next year he had 'an amazing experience'. He tasted La Rioja Alta's Vina Ardanza 1964 and realised that top-notch wine existed outside Bordeaux and Burgundy (a fact acknowledged by remarkably few of his peers 20 years ago).

On holiday in California in 1973 he could hardly believe the quality of wine made there (compared with the produce of Europe in its pre-technological age). Cullens customers were soon introduced to names such as Robert Mondavi and Christian Brothers.

He would always taste and then try to put a price on a given wine. 'If I could still make a margin on it, then I'd buy it' was his philosophy, regardless of the French Or Nothing mindset then prevailing. Thus two years later Rogers was the first stockist of a cheap Argentine wine (branded Franchette by its importers, presumably in the vain hope that less open-minded customers would not notice its outlandish origins).

And then in 1979 Rogers tasted the most extraordinary Cabernet Sauvignon bargain: a deep, fruity red that had all the punch lacking in so much cheap claret and was available by the tankerload from...Bulgaria, a place most customers would need an atlas to locate. 'It was fascinating how that became so successful,' remembers Rogers. 'I told all the shop managers to tell their claret-loving customers to serve it in a decanter and see what their friends thought of it. They loved it.'

Bottles from Australia and New Zealand followed in 1981 and Rogers became the first non-scribe individual to win an important award for spreading the wine gospel to the consumer – appropriately enough, from Marques de Cáceres, an innovative rioja producer. And then in 1985 Cullens was taken over.

Since then Rogers has been a consultant for importers Enotria Wines and the Barnes Wine Shop, has written for *Off-Licence News*, devised wine courses, and has been very ill. At one stage he could not even drink but continued to make wine judgments with confidence using only his nose. 'I'm surprised more people don't taste on the basis of smell alone; it gives the last wine as fair a chance as the first' reflects his philosophy towards both wine and illness fairly accurately.

But his tastes in wine continue to evolve, as of course does the world's wine output. 'I have had a love affair with rioja, with New Zealand Sauvignon, with Australian Chardonnay (I remember a Brown Brothers 1978 that made me think that the Aussies were going to rule the world), but I have come back to finesse. You can't beat the

French for sheer finesse, just as you can't beat the mystique attached to their labels.

'I'd love to observe two otherwise identical dinner parties where one lot of people is told they'll be served a first growth claret, and the other lot are just given it in a decanter without comment. I bet you'd get two completely different reactions.' This is typical of someone who cares deeply about what really is inside each bottle rather than its external baggage.

In his wine merchant existence, Rogers may have argued that, compared with the nose, the eye is virtually redundant. But in the last year or so he has harnessed his own eyes to a camera to such good effect that an exhibition of his photographs is being held at Newton's restaurant, 33 Abbeville Road. London SW4 (0181 673 0977). All proceeds go to a fund established by Rogers for those who nurse the terminally ill at St Mary's Hospital, Paddington.

November 27, 1993

James Rogers died five days after the publication of this article.

DURABLE ISLAND MAGIC

How very boring we all are. For 99 out 100 drinkers, wine is either red or white, very occasionally pink, and, if stronger than average, then invariably either sherry or port. But what about madeira (or 'm'darer' as it is called by those more intimate with the eponymous Atlantic island than I)?

Here is yet another world-famous wine invented by British merchants, and one that is truly thrilling to taste, yet it is all but ignored by the world's wine-drinkers. In Britain, for example, our imports of madeira are barely one fortieth of our imports of port.

I was reminded of the thrill of top quality madeira the other day as I wallowed in a wine made when Emily Brontë was four years old - a Cossart Gordon Verdelho 1822. It was a light tawny, beautifully creamy, mellow and probably nearing its prime but still lively enough to show off, being full and rich without too much sugar or alcohol but with madeira's characteristic tang. A prancing 171 year old! They say, and I've said too, that fino sherry's the thing to get the gastric juices flowing, but madeira does the same thing while offering the richness of a tawny port.

The great thing about madeira of any age or quality, unlike any other wine, is that you can open a bottle and sip at the contents for months before it starts to deteriorate. The bottles from which I tasted 18 vintage madeiras from 1971 back to 1822 the other day had been opened nearly two months previously and showed not a jot of decay.

But madeira has one more unique attribute in my experience. Compared with port, brandy or liqueurs - its rivals as what are ludicrously known as 'digestifs' - madeira is much less likely to cause a hangover. This is a bold claim. (On no account try this out at home, children, for madeira is almost half as strong as gin and has to be treated with caution.) But madeira does have a certain way of cleaning out the cerebral rafters before the morning after, when other drinks seem to leave a pile of old rubbish behind.

Not surprisingly perhaps, the finer the madeira, the more marked this effect, or rather lack of it. Vintage madeira is the most expensive of all, and is not even released before it is 20 years old, although it will still be in its infancy then. A bottle of vintage madeira is unlikely to cost much less than £60, but it can be sipped over many an evening, and makes a great birthday present if the year can be matched to recipient.

Madeira also produces historic wines made by fractional blending, so called solera madeiras dated with the year in which the blending system or solera was begun, typically in the 19th century. Not so useful for matching birth years perhaps, these can also be very fine, mature wines at much the same price as vintage madeiras.

Madeira was one of the first 'varietal' wines, traditionally made from a single grape variety in the following styles:

     Sercial - lightest, most delicately tangy and slowest maturing of all.
     Verdelho - Rather nuttier and fuller but still quite dry.
     Bual -Rich raisin and molasses flavours.
     Malmsey - The Malvasia grape makes the sweetest, darkest madeira.

The island's supply of these noble varieties has been so decimated by pests and diseases that today's basic three year old madeiras (labelled 'Finest', with blatant disregard for the English language) are made mainly from the lesser Tinta Negra Mole vine and are labelled stylistically rather than varietally, as in Dry, Medium Dry etc.

Five year old 'Reserve' blends are generally about £10, and should contain at least 85 per cent of the noble variety specified, but much better value are Special and Extra Reserves, older blends at £13 to £20 with more cask ageing and subtlety. Although vintage and solera madeiras are usually even better value than these 10 and 15 year old blends, some of the best madeira buys of all are the Reserve blends from Henriques & Henriques which have an average age of 88 years. Because they are not dated, they are available from La Vigneronne of London SW7, Britain's greatest cache of fine madeira, at the relatively sniplike price of £26.95 a bottle. Thresher/Bottoms Up/Wine Rack have also persisted with this unfashionable wine.

Since Portugal joined the EU, and the famous port family Symington took over control of most of the best known madeira names, the madeira wine industry is being licked into some sort of Euro-acceptable shape, but the wines live so long that it could be at least a century before every bottle of madeira in commercial circulation fits in to the neat, new taxonomy.

Drink these marvellous wines before and after meals, or with cheese, and revel in their durability. The 1964 and 1954 vintages are nowhere near ready.

Where to buy madeira:
Corney & Barrow of London EC1 0171-251 4051 and Newmarket
Farr Vintners of London SW1 0171-828 1960
Fortnum & Mason of London SW1 0171-734 8000
Great Northern Wine Co of Leeds 01532 461200
Patrick Grubb of Steeple Aston, Oxon 01869 340229
Justerini & Brooks of London SW1 0171-258 5000 and Edinburgh
Reid Wines of Hallatrow near Bristol 01761 452645
T & W of Thetford, Norfolk 01842 765646
La Vigneronne of London SW7 0171-589 6113

February 19, 1994

FINE WINE IN HEIDI COUNTRY

I f you go to the trouble of tracking down a bevy of beautiful wines made in minute quantities with impeccable fastidiousness in a Swiss cowshed, you expect a certain exclusivity on your story. But the longer I spent with Daniel Gantenbein, the more I realised I was treading in the footsteps of wine luminaries by the score.

Paul Draper, master winemaker of California's Ridge Vineyards, had apparently been to this corner of eastern Switzerland last summer, and communicated in the Italian familiar to Daniel from his holidays in Piedmont (where he rents a small vineyard to Elio Altare).

Gantenbein wines may be difficult to track down even 50 miles to the north-west in Zurich, but they can be found on the list at Piedmont's famous Da Guido restaurant, as well as in the more notable local restaurants and those immediately north in Liechtenstein. They may try to export to the US.

When I raved about the quality of his Riesling-Sylvaner 1992, I was told that that was the wine of which Ernst Loosen, whizzkid of the Mosel, had ordered a case.

And in Daniel's personal wine cellar, hollowed out of the slate underpinning of his native village of Fläsch, were all the names one would wish for oneself: Bordeaux's great names, Ponsot 1990 red burgundies, a tranche of Domaine de la Romanée-Conti, Guigal, Ridge, and a gaggle of bottles from the Mosel's Grosse Ring aristocracy. Daniel is the only producer of the Grosse Ring's own raw material in his area. 'For me Riesling, with Chardonnay, is *the* white grape variety'.

This small wine region in eastern, German-speaking Switzerland is the vinous heart of Graubünder canton, the Herrschaft. It produces predominantly simple, sweetish Blauburgunder (the Pinot Noir of Burgundy, of which the Mariafeld clone is widely revered here) together with Alsace's white grape varieties, MüllerThurgau and Completer, an eye-watering local curiosity.

The local market (truly local; the wines are almost unknown in French-speaking Switzerland) sustains relatively high prices here. Vines are planted amid pasture and all sorts of crops, but viticulture is the most profitable agricultural activity in this dramatically beautiful corner of Switzerland, through which thousands of skiers hurtle each weekend en route for Klosters and Davos.

The twinkling, energetic Daniel was until relatively recently a mechanic, and is still a meticulous craftsman, whether in winemaking or restoring his ancient farmhouse. After his wife Martha had qualified in viticulture, he studied wine-making, both at the local wine school in Wädenswil and nosing around producers he admires.

Since 1980 they have farmed a just-manageable total of four hectares (10 acres) of vines, on well exposed slopes below a vertiginous cliff face that leads the way to the Vorarlberg. The land is dissected by narrow open lanes, a rickety tractor wide.

Why are Gantenbein wines such a discernible cut above the rest? There is his infatuation with and exposure to the fine wines of the world (last year he and some friends had organised a wine tasting which culminated in a 1899 Montrachet).

There is also his practical determination to get things right. He bottles, for example, much later than most. The Herrschaft is currently in the grip of barrique worship, not always to the benefit of the resulting wines. Daniel has filled every corner of his winery with top quality French oak casks, but he experimented before deciding that double-sized barriques give the right wood-to-fruit ratio for his grapes.

And then there are, of course, the grapes themselves and, perhaps most importantly, the low yields encouraged by Martha in the vineyard, much lower than the Swiss norm.

Gantenbein Blauburgunder tastes like serious red wine with a future, the product of a minimal intervention winemaking policy. It is not surprising that it commands a 50 per cent premium on the going rate for the region of 12 Swiss francs per bottle.

But the much rarer white wines are possibly even more distinguished. Daniel's Weissburgunder 1990 was picked with a potential alcohol level of 13 per cent and was fermented cool and long ('just long enough to make people angry'). It is probably the best Pinot Blanc I have yet tasted. Perhaps it is inevitable that Daniel makes a Chardonnay (25 Swiss francs a bottle) but so does the rest of the world. No-one else I know makes a rich, red wine like the mystery he produced at the end of my tasting in his house.

It was very dark and dramatically concentrated, with lovely spicy fruit. Because we had been discussing the new concentrators that are being employed in Bordeaux to make claret more intense, I half-seriously suggested that this was the product of a concentrator.

His eyes lit up. 'Come downstairs and I'll show you my concentrator', he smiled, scampering down a dark staircase to a whitewashed chamber, windows open to the village street. Here were stacked wooden fruit boxes full of Pinot Noir grapes drying and sweetening, in imitation of the Italian passito technique used to produce Recioto and Amarone. This extraordinary hybrid of a wine sells at auction for more than 200 Swiss francs a half, which must go some way towards subsidising the Ponsots resting quietly next door.

March 19, 1994

HOLLYWOOD COMES TO COONAWARRA

I t was a marvellously unlikely scene for such a remote corner of South Australia. On a specially constructed platform above a sea of vines, two dozen Australian men, muted by the double indignity of wearing both ties and make-up, sat at tables whose fancy white tablecloths flapped in the breeze of a Coonawarra sunset.

Some had flown thousands of miles across the outback to participate in the sixth Wynnsday, an annual triumph of wine marketing. On a Wednesday each March (the Australian pronunciation of Wednesday being, almost exactly, 'Wynnsday') the new vintage of Wynns Coonawarra Estate wines is launched throughout Australia with simultaneous tastings in each of the six major cities, linked and broadcast by satellite.

A bank of television cameras between the vines and assorted Australian wine pundits transmitted their views on the Wynns 1991 range to the nation, or at least to the 4,000 wine enthusiasts and retailers who had assembled for similar tastings in hotel ballrooms around the country. 'G'day, Brisbane. What's your question for our winemaker Peter Douglas?' was a typical link.

Wynns, as its slogan continues to remind the avid Australian wine drinking public, is 'The Estate that made the Coonawarra world famous'. It is not the oldest but it was the Wynn family who saved the region from reverting to sheep farming by demonstrating its extraordinary affinity with Cabernet Sauvignon grapes in the 1950s and 1960s, when the Australian wine market was still dominated by things sweet and sticky.

Today, the Wynns themselves make Mountadam, Eden Ridge and David Wynn wines 250 miles north in the Eden Valley, while Wynns Coonawarra Estate is part of the giant Southcorp group, whose other core businesses include packaging and water heater manufacture.

Southcorp Wines Pty, recently renamed, controls about a third of all Australian wine production, including such names as Penfolds, Lindemans, Seppelt, Tollana, Wynns, Seaview, Leo Buring, Killawarra, Rouge Homme and a host of other familiar names. (The group does not like apostrophes.)

In Coonawarra alone - an extraordinary island of particularly suitable, well-drained, fertile terra rossa, the remains of an ancient coral reef, less than 10 miles long and hardly a mile across - Southcorp owns not just Wynns, which is in the happy position of owning a third of the region's vineyards, but through its other subsidiaries controls by far the dominant share of the country's most prized, virtually unextendable, wine region.

Just down the road (and there really is only one road) from Wynns are the Lindemans and Rouge Homme wines, made at a quite distinct winery, and Penfolds' 600 acres of Coonawarra vines (as well as a recent distribution agreement with the extensive Katnook estate). The remarkable feature of Southcorp wine policy is that each of these subsidiaries and close neighbours is run in fierce competition with each other. Differences in vine growing and wine making techniques are positively encouraged.

All Southcorp vineyards in this underpopulated area are heavily mechanised, however (like those of all but a handful of growers such as Petaluma) and are characterised by widely spaced rows of rampant vines. This smooths out annual variations in yields, but satisfies the company's accountants more than wine critics.

The fertile terra rossa sells for up to A$1,500 an acre (twice as much as land one mile east or west). Houses therefore continue to be razed, and Lindemans, for example, solves the problem of a small and disappearing workforce by 'minimal' pruning, leaving the fruit to find its own way out to the light from a tangle of canes on about a third of its top vineyards Pyrus, Limestone Ridge and St George. Each of these is described dolefully as a 'finite resource', a relatively new viticultural concept in Australia.

Southcorp is continuing a commitment to producing a wide and competing range of top quality wines that is unusual in a wine company of this size, however. Since the 1960s Penfolds has been proud of its in-house legend in the form of Penfolds Grange, a deep, rich red described famously by Hugh Johnson in the 1970s as 'Australia's one first growth'.

Since then winemakers throughout the group (whose ownership and constitution have been in constant evolution) have been worked hard to produce rivals for Grange, bottles for Aussies to fight over, such as the Lindemans single vineyard wines. Wynns' nominee was launched with the 1982 vintage as John Riddoch Cabernet Sauvignon, an intense and rapturously received essence of Coonawarra from Wynns' oldest vineyards.

It was joined on last year's Wynnsday by Michael Hermitage 1990 (although under the terms of the recent bilateral trade agreement with Europe it will eventually have to be renamed Michael Shiraz). This incredible hulk is already selling at A$80 a bottle. Wynns' phones were buzzing last Wynnsday with customers begging to increase their allocations of the Michael Hermitage 1991 released that day at around A$38 a bottle.

Tiny quantities of Michael Shiraz (which should be aged for a good 10 years) should reach Oddbins by the beginning of June and will sell for about £15. But Wynns' real bargain, and a wine probably better suited to the more modest dimensions of the average European palate, is the black label Wynns Coonawarra Estate Cabernet Sauvignon.

The handsome 1988 and ripe 1990 are currently £7.99 at Oddbins and Victoria Wine, and will be followed by the 1991, a truly fine, beautifully balanced wine designed not to impress, but to express, Coonawarra.

Peter Douglas, Wynns' incredible winemaking hulk, has wrought miracles since he arrived in 1985. Southcorp's divide-and-rule policy, however, means that he and winemaker Sue Hodder strive to see some of the wine produced at Wynns Coonawarra Estate selected as an ingredient in, say, Penfolds Grange. Penfolds Bin 707 Cabernet Sauvignon depends particularly heavily on Wynns input.

Only about 40 per cent of the 18,000 tonnes of grapes crushed this year at the distinctive three-gabled winery illustrated on each label of Wynns Coonawarra Estate will be bottled under that name. It also vinifies the produce of Southcorp's substantial, and expanding, vineyard holdings in the rest of this usefully cool south east corner of South Australia, Padthaway in particular.

On Wynnsday the winery was processing early-picked Pinot Noir grapes en route to the Southcorp sparkling wine plant at Great Western over the border in Victoria. Truckloads of grapes had also been shipped down from the heavily irrigated Riverland 200 miles north when rot threatened the crop if it waited until the local Southcorp winery was ready for it. This is how big can be beautiful in the wine business.

April 9, 1994

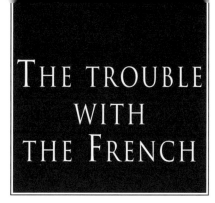

THE TROUBLE WITH THE FRENCH

Wine is one of the great strengths of France. The name Margaux or Lafite is much better known around the world than, say, Balladur, but the French seem to take no pride at all in their wines. Britain has much better media coverage of the subject. French newspaper and book editors aren't interested in French wine writers. You have to be British or American to get published.

'The quality of a new vintage is a very important cultural and economic fact to France but, contrary to any other subject, reporters never ask an independent outsider about it. They ask the Ministry of Agriculture!'

The exasperated 'independent outsider' delivering this diatribe is Michel Bettane, widely hailed as France's top, if underutilised, wine writer. A jolly ovoid, vintage 1952, self-taught and passionately devoted to wine quality, he gave up teaching classics three years ago to devote himself full time to the French monthly magazine *Revue du Vin de France* (RVF) of which he is not editor but its trump card. Although France is the world's leading wine producer, RVF is France's only consumer publication devoted to wine. Britain has at least three (*Decanter*, *WINE* and *The Vine*) while *Wine Spectator*, *The Wine Advocate*, *Wine Enthusiast*, *Appellation* and the *Quarterly Review of Wine* are just some of their American counterparts.

The approaches and objectives of these three countries' wine writers could hardly be more different. For Bettane, it is as important to inform and guide France's hundreds of thousands of vine growers as the wine consumers among RVF's 30,000 readers. His particular hobby horses are the need to limit yields, the evils of relying on a single clone of each vine variety, and the virtues of ecologically sensitive viticulture.

He accordingly spends at least three months each year in vineyards and cellars virtually counselling his vigneron buddies. His reference points for each vintage include Michel Delon, Alain Vauthier and Michel Rolland in Bordeaux and Lafon, Leflaive, Leroy and Accad in Burgundy.

Famed for both his palate and his memory, he never takes a note in situ. 'It's just a matter of politesse: you're a guest; a grower gives you what he thinks is his best wine. How can people do it? What's more important is to listen to the wine and to the grower.'

His policy is to criticise by omission rather than to publish a poor review. 'It is very important to say the truth to the growers, but not necessarily to the readers'. When asked how he retains his objectivity, he interprets the question as referring to his personal tasting technique rather than any suggestion of partiality.

American wine writers, on the other hand, will do anything to maintain their distance from producers. The preferred research method of America's influential Robert Parker, for example, is to assemble and compare hundreds of sample bottles on neutral territory. Comments and points out of 100 based on his palate rather than any contact with individual producers are then printed in ruthless detail.

While most American wine writers concentrate on nosing out the finest and rarest (and often most expensive) wines, the British approach is more democratic, but can be considerably less inspiring. 'Go there, buy that' succinctly summarises the average British wine article. British wine journalism is still informed by the notion that the writer's job is demystify this curious foreign beast called wine and swell the ranks of wine drinkers. The chief beneficiaries of this are the supermarkets, and those selling wines under £4 a bottle.

In France, Bettane sees his job as halting the decline of wine consumption overall in France, and educating a new generation of consumers who are more aware than their forebears of how little they know about wine.

While Britain's consumerist wine writers list retail stockists, their American counterparts have to limit themselves to specifying importers, so complex is the US distribution system.

Bettane and his ilk simply give the address of the producer, however. 'In France we don't have wine merchants, and those few cavistes that exist have no knowledge at all of the international wine market.'

As well as travelling to the US and possibly Italy or Germany once a year, Bettane reads the British and American wine press avidly. He treasures his relationship with 'Bob' (like Parker, Bettane was born in Maryland during his father's Washington posting) even though they differ on the subject of wine scores out of 100. 'They are very, very dangerous. More and more the wine trade simply reacts to these points rather than knowing what they like and want to sell.

'I have resisted publishing points in RVF. We use a much more general star system. In France we judge in a more cultural, civilised way. To understand Pinot Noir, for example, you must understand the culture of Pinot Noir before the technical knowledge.

'No Frenchman knows more about California or Italian wines than me but it's difficult to write about them because there's no market for them in France - although more French people are becoming interested in non-French wines, especially Italian wines because of the cuisine.

'I think California produces some superb wines, but Australians? I just cannot understand them. Even someone as sympathetic as James Halliday [Australia's top wine writer and a wine producer] seems to be from another planet. Acids, tannins, balance, we taste completely differently. With Davis [the academic centre of California wine], I understand them - and I know they're wrong. With Australians, I can't even understand them.'

For the moment, however, Bettane has quite enough problems to sort out at home. 'We think that more than 60, perhaps 80, per cent of all French appellation contrôlée wines are below the necessary level of quality, especially in Burgundy and Champagne. That's why vins de pays producers deserve success; because they work so much harder. Perhaps the best value appellations in general are in south west France - Madiran, Jurançon, Bergerac and the Languedoc. They are modern wines with the complexity of French tradition rather than the simplicity of the New World. And,' here he gives his trademark mischievous smile', 'they're so much less boring than Bordeaux.'

May 14, 1994

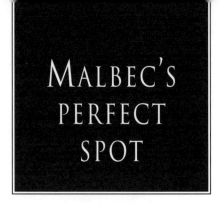

MALBEC'S PERFECT SPOT

I f ever there were proof that every grape variety has its perfect place, then Mendoza Malbec is it. In the rest of the world Malbec is hardly one of the great grapes. Once widely grown in Bordeaux, it is now effectively known only in Cahors, where it is called Cot or Auxerrois, and generally turns out rather tough, charmless, essentially country wines - despite the millions of francs poured into Cahors by well-heeled Parisians and New Yorkers pursuing a vineyard hobby. It may take the recently arrived chef Alain Senderens to show us otherwise.

In the higher temperatures and richer soils of Mendoza, however, Argentina's main wine-making province just east of the Andes, Malbec seems to luxuriate. The wines it produces are lush, rich, heavily spiced and yet the best of them have quite enough acid and tannin to make them appetising bets for long term ageing.

Not that Malbec is at all revered in Argentina. It is one of the cheapest red grape varieties, commanding considerably less of a price than the more glamorous Merlot and Cabernet Sauvignon perhaps because it sounds less obviously French, especially when spelt Malbeck, as it often is in Argentina. And in the vast domestic wine market (about the same size as that of the entire United States), French names enjoy the greatest cachet, no matter how far fetched.

Carcassonne, for example, is the irrelevant name of a popular blend of Cabernet and Malbec, while its sister blend of Malbec, Merlot and Syrah is called after that singularly smelly cheese Pont l'Evêque.

Malbec's ubiquity in Mendoza doubtless militates against its glorification. For long it was the most planted red wine grape (although a vine pull scheme has led to its being overtaken by a grape called Bonarda, which may be the same as California's Charbono).

Parts of Mendoza can be extremely hot, as witness the ancient plane trees which flank so many of the main roads, but Luján de Cuyo to the south of Mendoza city (with Vistalba the highest sub-district) seems to offer perfect conditions for Malbec. At an altitude of about 900 m (nearly as high as Switzerland's highest vineyard, for example), it can offer suitably cool nights even in late summer.

With unlimited sunshine and unlimited irrigation water from the Andes (already sporting their first fall of snow last March), Mendoza has been one of the world's most productive wine facto-ries since Spaniards and Italians settled here in the late 19th cen-tury - although oil has since become a more important product in the province.

Mendoza's major natural disadvantage is its minute annual rainfall of about 180mm (500mm is generally considered a viticultural minimum without irrigation), of which about 150mm falls at harvest time, often in the devastating form of hail. Growers just have to reck-on on sacrificing between 10 and 20 per cent of each year's crop to the capricious clouds on their side of the Andes.

Raul de la Motta of Weinert, 'the small winery producing big wines' from carefully bought in grapes, has made more than 50 vin-tages here and is one of the few Argentines to recognise that Malbec might be the Argentine wine industry's trump card.

'The whole world makes Cabernet, but with Malbec, our wines have distinction. Malbec ages very well here.' He can demonstrate the gamey, wild animal smells of young Malbec as well as the mellow-er, richer characters of Malbec aged for more years than would be thought wise in France in the giant old oak vats that characterise this wine industry ripe for renovation.

Weinert believes in blending Malbec, which with Cabernet forms about a third of their delicious Cavas Weinert blend, exported to the UK and US, and most of their bargain-priced Carrascal for the domestic market.

In neighbouring Agrelo, (Moët &) Chandon (whose 'Comte de Beltour' is another bargain blend of Merlot, Malbec and Syrah) have been experimenting with ageing Malbec (and Cabernet, and of course Chardonnay) in small French oak barriques, with aromatic, juicy, well structured results. They are launching these new fangled varietals in Argentina under the name of the winery's first oenologist. Fortunately, for marketing reasons anyway, he was called Renaud Poirier rather than Reg Pratt.

A new anglo-saxon name on the Argentine wine map, how-ever, is Peter Bright, the Portugal-based Australian winemaker who has been cooking up some fine blends on behalf of the British super-market Sainsbury's at Peñaflor/Trapiche, Argentina's biggest producer, also based in Mendoza. For long a champion of Portugal's rich heritage of native grape varieties, Bright was quick to see the potential of Malbec, and Bright Brothers' Malbec 1992 Las Palmas should be well worth seeking out at £5.45 in 60 of Sainsbury's larger stores from early June.

Other, forward-looking winemakers who have discovered that Mendoza Malbec has an affinity with small oak barrels include Alberto Arizu at Luigi Bosca, who is actively looking for importers for fine wines which include his 1991 Malbec from 40 year-old vines; Nieto y Senetiner/Valle de Vistalba/Santa Isabel (exported to Switzerland); and Bodega Norton, into which vast sums are being poured by the Swarovski family of Austria. But that is another story.

June 18, 1994

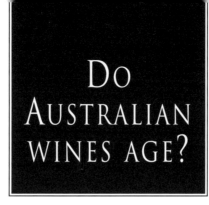

DO AUSTRALIAN WINES AGE?

There seems to be some sort of tax on showing emotion in Australia. Certainly Australian winemakers are the most phlegmatic in the world, and Rosemount's Philip Shaw is a prime example. Earlier this summer, in his usual, heavy-lidded monotone, he presented the first 11 vintages of his pride and joy, Roxburgh Chardonnay, in a suite as opulent as the wine itself at the Ritz Hotel in London. "Quite a nice wine" was about as close as he got to enthusiasm, even about the intense and unashamedly Hunter Roxburgh Chardonnay 1993 .

The wines took us on a textbook trip through the recent history of the world's favourite grape variety in Australia, with the younger vintages substantially outshining those made before 1987.

This was back in the Dark Chardonnay Ages when winemakers thought that lots of new oak and deliberate avoidance of oxidation during winemaking was the answer. All that happened was that the deep golden wine all too often turned brown and flat in bottle at about three years old.

From 1987 Shaw, arguably Australia's most influential arbiter of Chardonnay winemaking fashion, used ambient rather than commercial yeasts, cut down on the sulphur dioxide and acid additions, and began to decrease the proportion of new oak.

Although the quality of Australian Chardonnay has increased almost immeasurably since the late 1980s, relatively few of them (Petaluma and Leeuwin?) have demonstrated the ability to age. Most are made, perhaps more sensibly, in the full knowledge that almost all Australian wine is drunk within a few hours of being bought.

The Cowra region in New South Wales has long provided some of the best fruit for this exuberantly fruity style of Chardonnay and The Rothbury Estate Cowra Chardonnay 1993, £5.95 at 100 Sainsbury stores, is a particularly fine example.

Grapes other than Chardonnay are a better bet for those with serious cellaring intentions. The best of the bevy of Australian Rieslings now available in Britain will age well, and Hunter Valley Semillon is a prime example of wine which actually needs years in bottle to show its best. Sainsbury's has the probably underpriced McWilliam's Mount Pleasant Elizabeth Semillon 1988 for £6.25 in their top 50 stores; it is not nearly ready to drink.

By historical fluke (ships refuelling at Madeira perhaps), Australia grows quite a bit of the long-lived, tangy white grape Verdelho, and producers are, fortunately for us, beginning to see its potential. Richmond Grove Verdelho 1993 is another exciting product of Cowra, from a Jacob's Creek affiliate, and costs about £6 from stockists which include Sainsbury's.

More handcrafted and subtle, however, is David Traeger's Nagambie Verdelho 1993, £6.99, from the state of Victoria via the Australian Wine Centre of London WC1. It has serious substance, no obvious added acid, slight nuttiness and a very slight fizz. It would make a great aperitif.

Australian reds have in general shown much better ageing potential than whites. A few days before the decade of Roxburgh, Australia's wine giant Penfolds showed off, inasmuch as Australians allow themselves to show off, historical ranges of some of their most popular red wines back to into the prehistory of the 1970s, and even a slightly decrepit bottle of Bin 60A 1962.

Every Grange back to 1976 was a turn-on in some respect; but it was the obvious ageability of their high volume lines such as Koonunga Hill and Bin 128 that was the most impressive result.

Koonunga Hill 1982 was an absolute delight at 12 years old - just the thing for the Bordelais who cannot believe that subtlety is ever to be found Down Under. In fact although the wine contains more Shiraz grapes than Cabernet (especially so in 1982 when Cabernet was all the rage and Shiraz an as yet uncelebrated resource), the wine had an uncannily Bordeaux-like balance and bouquet.

The 1982 was a museum bottle but Koonunga Hill Shiraz-Cabernet 1992, widely distributed at £5-something, is both very easy to drink now and should keep well. In contrast, Penfolds Bins 128 Coonawarra Shiraz seemed a less successful candidate for the cellar. The 1991 is still quite hard work because of the acid that manages to dominate its big, fat fruit, while the 1986 was still chewy but a bit simple, and the 1980 was old rather than mature.

The Wine Society of Stevenage have an Australian red that is currently at a delightful stage of well-mannered, drinkable middle age: Houghton Gold Reserve 1988 is £5.95 and comes from the Margaret River on the cool southern tip of Western Australia.

Its maker would probably describe it as "not a bad drink". I would call it gorgeous.

August 27, 1994

ANOTHER RAINY SEPTEMBER?

The general store in Meursault, Burgundy's quintessential white wine village, has its usual vintage-time window display: piles of secateurs, rows of giant vacuum jugs, Musti-metres, and rubber boots. This year, it is the rubber boots that have been most in demand, while the Musti-metres, for on-the-spot measurements of grape sugar levels, have had a depressing tale to tell.

The vineyards are a mire. The pickers are wearing mud-spattered oilskins and rubber gloves. The village streets throb with tractors pulling loads of sodden grapes all too often tinged brown with rot, covered with tarpaulins in an attempt to keep at least the last hour's drizzle from diluting the juice, and therefore the wine.

An evening walk around the backstreets of Meursault reveals medieval courtyard after courtyard sodden with mud. The village acoustic is the sound of a heavy duty hose desperately trying to keep the wine presses, the trailers and the hods clean. The mood is sombre.

Burgundy, like the rest of France, enjoyed an unusually hot summer. At the end of August the grapes were riper and healthier than usual. It seemed as though this could be just the vintage France needed, but farmers such as these know better than to bank on the weather. In the first week of September the rain set in, and continued almost daily, to make this the most miserable vintage since 1984 according to optimists, since 1947 according to pessimists.

The French wine industry badly needs a top quality wine harvest, if only for its morale. Wine consumption in France has been plummeting, and French wine exports have fallen nearly 20 per cent in the last five years as other countries have presented an increasing threat to France's viticultural supremacy. France badly needs some of the sunshine which most New World wine producers take for granted.

It is now four years since the last seriously good vintage in Burgundy, Bordeaux and the Rhône to generate excitement about

French wines. Too many of France's lesser wines lack the 'punch' (for which in many cases read sun-generated alcohol) that New World wines use to seduce new wine consumers).

France today is better at the technical business of winemaking than it has ever been, but the acceleration rate elsewhere, particularly in the New World and also in Spain and Italy, has been even more impressive. Besides, many modern consumers seem to favour the New World's 'varietal' approach whereby wines are named after the grape varieties from which they are made to France's much more complicated geographical naming.

There will probably be some good white wines, for rot is by no means disastrous for white grapes and the acidity levels will please those of us who like our white wine without puppy fat. The best sites and best-kept vineyards such as Dominique Lafon's Meursault-Perrières can boast tiny, relatively healthy grapes which should yield modest amounts of concentrated wine, but the 1994 vintage will be a real trial for France's less skilled winemakers, of which there are still too many.

It is the red grapes which will take the strain of all this rain, particularly where yields are high. Rot destroys pigment and the skins so necessary to red winemaking can taint the final wine. This will be one of those (many) vintages about which wine trade will be able to boast "the strictest selection is necessary; buy only from a reputable merchant such as ourselves". Those who are already practising 'organic' and even 'biodynamic' chemical-free vine-growing techniques are boasting of markedly healthier grapes than their neighbours in these damp conditions. One prominent example is Lalou Bize-Leroy, 'the queen of Burgundy', whose vineyards this year were treated not only to ground nettles applied according to phases of the moon but also to various tisanes applied from a helicopter.

Her traditional wooden open-topped fermentation vats (computer controlled) are full of healthy, small bunches of Pinot Noir grapes which will doubtless become yet another vintage of Domaine Leroy bottles the world's collectors will argue over.

A new development in Burgundy is the two-wheeled tourist. Cycling through Burgundy, on carefully pre-arranged and annotated routes from one three star hotel to another seems to have become a popular American vacation. This year streams of well-dressed cyclists were directed through the world-famous vineyards of the Domaine de la Romanée-Conti, no matter how muddy.

On Wednesday, when this vintage's combination of frenzy and gloom was at its peak, a small group of cyclists was to be seen wheeling disconsolately round the courtyard of the Domaine des Comtes Lafon, mystified that no-one would find the time to sell them a bottle or two of Lafon's world-famous Meursaults.

Meanwhile mud-spattered, low-paid pickers who had been working in the sodden vineyards since 7.30a.m. stomped towards their lunch and Lafon Rosé de Saignée 1993. *They* were being paid to expend their calories between one dinner and the next.

The tourists who have been trudging round France's wine regions in the rain, or loitering longer than they would choose in their hotel rooms, may also be miserable, but at least for them it is just one damp holiday. For the vignerons the loss may be in their income and, in some cases, their reputation.

September 26, 1994

A SOUR TASTE IN HERMITAGE

Does France's oldest wine region need an *enfant terrible*? Almost certainly not, but never mind, Michel Chapoutier shows no signs of either growing up or calming down, which makes life for the rest of us extremely entertaining. His neighbouring vine growers on the famous, vine-covered hill of Hermitage in the northern Rhône Valley just south of Lyons are less amused. Indeed the atmosphere in the tiny, wine-dominated town of Tain l'Hermitage, where all but one of the famous names of the Rhône are based, has become distinctly vinegary.

The trouble with young Chapoutier, who took over this substantial family business from his father as recently as 1989, is that what he makes up for in fervour, he lacks in statesmanship. He is diminutive, wears a swot's pebble glasses, has a rare passion for irony and visibly tries, invariably unsuccessfully, to control his tongue.

He is utterly besotted with biodynamism, the Steiner-inspired farming techniques which involve regenerating the soil in harmony with astrology. He is also convinced that low yields are the key to wine quality, and usually accompanies his tasting notes with impressively low hectolitre-per-hectare statistics.

Michel Chapoutier is equally convinced, however, that most other producers in the northern Rhône (including his father Max) have got it wrong, and rarely misses an opportunity to point this out.

Things came to a head this summer when the influential American wine critic Robert Parker, clearly much taken with the intensely concentrated 'new' Chapoutier style, printed Michel's complaints that during the difficult, wet 1993 growing season the chemicals used by neighbouring vine-growers affected the margins of his vineyards, leaving them vulnerable to the fungal diseases which ravaged many non-biodynamic vineyards.

The result was an intemperate letter to Parker from the crème de la crème of Hermitage, including Gérard Jaboulet, Chave, and Delas, vilifying Chapoutier, claiming that his Hermitage vineyard had in fact been treated with weedkiller, and had been sprayed by helicopter. These other growers also included some figures which suggested that Chapoutier's average yields were considerably higher than he claimed.

Now Michel Chapoutier himself has issued his response in this dispute between the most prominent inhabitants of Tain l'Hermitage (population 5,000), all of whom work cheek by jowl. He must have chuckled at the helicopter accusation, for of course there is nothing esentially anti-organic about heli-spraying indeed the fanatical Lalou Bize-Leroy, 'the queen of Burgundy', applied several tisanes by helicopter to her world-famous vineyards last year.

The weedkiller claim is furiously rejected by Chapoutier and described as one of the most serious. His reply also contains some laborious play with statistics, notably with red and white wine areas as factors, to demonstrate that Chapoutier's yields in Hermitage were a relatively modest 33.15 hl/ha in 1993 (in Châteauneuf-du-Pape just 20.46 hl/ha).

The rain which also dogged this year's harvest in the northern Rhône is unlikely to wash away the issues involved in this dispute, however. Gérard Chave describes Chapoutier's response as "Unbelievable. I have never seen anything like this in the whole of my professional life."

Chapoutier acknowledges in his reply that he is widely criticized for being young and passionate, and claims that it is precisely his youth which spurs him on to take a long term view, embracing the wholemeal methods and low yields which he believes will preserve the good name of France's great wine appellations.

What is interesting, he points out in conclusion, is to ponder the real motivation of his angry neighbours? With the irritating tunnel vision of any young revolutionary, he suggests they are propelled by fear of these 'new' techniques, and the sacrifices that will be necessary to implement them.

In modern viticulture, radicalism means a return to traditional roots, a rejection of the commercial agrochemistry which has transformed vineyards in the last three decades. In winemaking too Chapoutier is notable for an attachment to ancient methods, particularly the much-photographed twice-daily pigeage, during which four muscly legs stomp down grape skins in the firm's unfashionably opentopped, wooden fermentation vats.

Certainly the new Chapoutier wines, from 1989 onwards, are impressive. They are refreshingly wild and intense (just like their maker), the sort of dense essences that require good cellaring and careful handling.

And they are available in the sort of quantities that propel all but the most limited bottlings into major distribution (Marks & Spencer even tried their hand with a Chapoutier Rasteau but it was far too risqué for them). Majestic, Oddbins, Thresher, Adnams of Southwold, Averys of Bristol, Gauntleys of Nottingham, Justerini & Brooks of London SW1 and Edinburgh and Tanners of Shrewsbury all stock some wines from the new regime.

What young Chapoutier needs is an advisor, less a Max Clifford than Marcel Guigal, the softly spoken wizard of Côte-Rôtie 40 minutes' drive upriver. "Calm down," has been his advice to all concerned.

October 22, 1994

Grape pickers droop

AUSTRIAN WINE - WHITER THAN WHITE

What German wine needs is a real humdinger of a scandal - widespread addition of antifreeze perhaps - and the will to take it seriously. The diethylene glycol debacle has certainly worked wonders for Austrian wine. Nearly 10 years on, with fundamentally revised legislation and painstaking quality control systems, the Austrian wine industry is so freshly scrubbed and cloaked in virtue it is almost blindingly bright, while the German wine business is still shrouded in the grey mists of compromise and rampant commercialism.

Fastidious American importers such as Vin DiVino of Chicago and Terry Theise of Milton S Kronheim & Co, Washington DC are fighting over Austria's top wine producers, blasting their customers with phrases such as "I gotta warn you: prepare to be surprised, 'cause you ain't never tasted stuff like dis".

The British wine trade is proceeding rather more sedately, as is its wont. In fact if it doesn't act soon it will find that the Americans, the Germans and even the Japanese (who import almost as much Austrian wine than the British) will have snapped up all the top wines. Austria suffers from the reverse problem to, say, Chile. It has ample evidence of producing some of the world's finest wines: dry Rieslings, from the Wachau and (often better value) neighbouring Kremstal and Kamptal; Styrian varietals of Collio-like purity; and the most luscious botrytised sweet wines from Burgenland. What it hasn't got is an ocean of seriously cheap plonk to lap at the shores of the supermarkets - except for an extraordinary new product called Servus.

Designed, very much designed, to sell at about £3 a bottle on British high streets, it is an attempt by the new governor of

Burgenland to shape some of his state's surplus supply of basic off-dry white into something that will sustain commercially viable viticulture in Burgenland, and tempt new wine drinkers to try Austria. Producer Lenz Moser, one of the very few big merchants to have survived the scandal, is gambling on its success, marketing it defiantly in a clear bordeaux bottle. It tastes crisp and utterly unobjectionable if undistinguished.

The economy and geography of Austria, however, are probably best suited to titillating connoisseurs. British wine drinkers prepared to spend £7 to £40 a bottle can find proof of Austria's uniquely dedicated new generation of wine producers at the addresses listed below.

The parallel between Austrian and German wine is obvious, not just because the label language and many of the grape varieties grown are the same, but because the German wine industry today faces many of the same problems faced by its Austrian counterpart in the early 1980s just before the glycol scandal enforced a clean sweep.

Large commercial bottlers have forced Germany's grape prices down to such an extent that German wines, which were prized above classed growth bordeaux at the turn of the century, are viewed by many as the lowest of the vinous low. We enthusiasts continue to wave a flag for Germany's quality-conscious producing elite, but the country's reputation continues to be damaged by the lax controls on what officially constitutes 'quality wine' (about 95 per cent of production).

In fact the so-called 'antifreeze scandal' of 1985 reflected just as badly on Germany than on Austria. This harmless additive was used exclusively by a limited number of Austrian merchants (not growers) to add body to sweet Austrian wine and was subsequently found in many bottles of supposedly 'German' wine. But the questions raised by this were never properly answered.

The Germans had a chance last year to reform their wine laws and they blew it. Enormously high yields are still permitted, and there was no radical reform of the complicated and often misleading nomenclature or the minimum ripeness levels required for each category. It is left to the better producers, such as (but by no means exclusively) those who belong to the VDP group, to impose their own higher standards.

For the moment, the consumer is left at the end of the queue but the future is bleak for any wine producer which ignores the consumer in today's market.

Some Austrian importers: Adnams of Southwold and T & W WInes of Thetford (01842 765646) for Willy Opitz' crazy half-bottlings; Noel Young of Trumpington (01223 844744) for Kracher sweet wines and Pöckl reds; Richard Nurick of Pangbourne (01734 842565) for Stiegelmar and Sonnhof; Lay & Wheeler of Colchester for some fine Styrian and Burgenland bottles; Richard Spiers Wines of Guildford (01483 37605) for a small Kremstal and Burgunland selection; Forth Wines of Milnathort (01577 862513) for some of Lenz Moser's estate bottlings; and Penistone Court Wine Cellars of Sheffield (01226 766037). Important wholesalers of fine Austrian wine include Caxton Tower of Brentford for Loiben, Fritz Salomon et al; and for some top quality dry Rieslings FWW Wines of Banstead (0181-786 8161) the new UK arm of the excellent co-operative at Dürnstein in the Wachau. Watch this space.

November 12, 1994

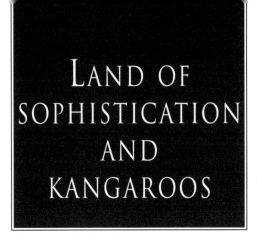

LAND OF SOPHISTICATION AND KANGAROOS

Just back from ten days in Australia and what sticks in my mind? The juiciest, fruitiest little oysters I've ever had in my life, from the west coast of South Australia and now feared as commercial rivals to the Sydney rock versions. A boned, spiced quail sitting on a couscous salad with fresh date chutney. Meltingly tender kangaroo fillet in chilli and black bean sauce...

Oh, and I believe I washed down Australia's dynamic new cuisine with the odd glass of wine - some of it just as exciting and mouldbreaking. In fact, come to think of it, I don't think I drank a single overtly oaky Chardonnay - the wine style with which the Australians wooed the now-infatuated British - the whole time I was there.

Australia continues to refine her wine styles. Over-oaked, heavy wines are becoming a thing of the past - in fact within Australia oak is now seen as an enemy to be tamed. Many wines are sold with the proud legend 'Unoaked' on the label, typically carrying a price premium above basic Chardonnay fruit given 'oak flavour' by oak chips rather than by maturation in barrels that can cost as much as A$1,000 apiece once they've been shipped here from France. (The Australian wine industry is one of the better customers of the American oak barrel business.)

Australia's new pride in its widely planted Shiraz (the Rhône's noble Syrah) has been a delight to behold - and I even got the faint impression that Cabernet Sauvignon was out of favour, although admittedly I spent most of my time in the Barossa Valley, Australia's Shirazshire.

Another noticeable trend is that Australia, like California, is developing its own band of Rhône Rangers, producers cherishing other vine varieties commonly (if in some cases erroneously) associated with France's Rhône Valley. As in California Grenache and Mataro (a.k.a. Mourvèdre) were scorned as cheap workhorse varieties for years, until their respective direct links with Châteauneuf-du-Pape and Bandol were recognised.

Today dry farmed (non irrigated) Grenache from the likes of Rockford and Turkey Flat (grape grower Peter Schulz's fruit made at Rockford) is offered with pride in the smarter restaurants of Adelaide, Sydney and Melbourne. Another cult wine is RBJ Theologicum, a gamey blend of Grenache and Mourvèdre from the Barossa (the 1993 is £7.49 from the Australian Wine Centre).

And was it my hopeful imagination or was Riesling actually making a comeback as opposed to being about to? These racy dry wines make a great alternative aperitif to champagne.

Certainly Australia is now a seriously useful source of well made sweet wines, typically about £7 a half bottle, that can, often should, be drunk young. They are not desperately popular in Australia itself and so it is up to us to encourage their producers to continue with this painstaking sideline.

In Britain there are still scores of beautifully made wines to be found in the price bracket Australia continues to do best, £5 to £10ish a bottle, and a high proportion of them are sold by the Australian Wine Centre (0800 716893).

WHITES

Primo Estate Colombard 1994 £5.99 AWC

Charmingly idiosyncratic wine made from a grape variety that is usually dull-as-ditch but in the hands of Joe Grilli (the 'Joseph' of the Moda Amarone listed below) these grapes ripened under the merciless sun of the Adelaide Plains become a full bodied, spicy, fruity dry white.

Stafford Ridge Lenswood Riesling 1991 £6.75 Adnams of Southwold, £6.99 AWC

Geoff Weaver releases his Riesling late, bless him, and here is the Adelaide Hills get to Alsace. Definitely dry (which not all Australians Rieslings are), long and kernel-scented.

Chapel Hill Eden Valley Riesling 1993 £6.49 AWC and Bottoms Up Pure, long, intensely aromatic.

St Hallett Chardonnay 1993 Tesco, Thresher etc £7.49

Big, broad Barossa style of Chardonnay but with enough subtlety to convince an extremely experienced Burgundian blind taster it was made with French and not American oak.

Ironstone Semillon Chardonnay £5.99 Majestic, Fullers, Cellar

5 Truly interesting south Western Australian that smells of tangy Semillon but has the weight of carefully grown Chardonnay - a less expensive label from Cape Mentelle.

Rothbury Hunter Valley Chardonnay 1993
Oddbins, Davisons £5.99 and Marco's shops around London

First class value for medal-winning liquid gold. Buy lots of this vintage; the Hunter is suffering dreadfully from drought.

Petaluma Chardonnay 1992 £9.99 Oddbins

Very good price for this level of sophistication from the cool Adelaide Hills. Great delicacy for the moment, but this one is worth hanging on to until the four to eight year-old 'drinking window' recommended by its made Brian Croser.

Shaw & Smith Reserve Chardonnay 1993 £10.99 Winecellars Textbook early 1990s barrel-fermented Chardonnay. Where will fashion take us from here - back to matchsticks in pineapple juice?

Henschke Croft Chardonnay 1992 £11.95 Lay & Wheeler of Colchester Savoury oak, appetising. A third fine Chardonnay from the Adelaide Hills.

Primo Estate Botrytis Riesling 1993 £7.99 a half AWC and Harvey Nichols London SW1

Pure but not for purists as this was made by inducing the botrytis mould at the winery rather than in the vineyard, but for me it's a delightfully racy sweet wine without the clout of a Griffith Semillon.

REDS
Peter Lehmann Vine Vale Shiraz 1992 £3.99

Okay, so it's less than £5 but don't complain, just enjoy the oomph.

Chateau Reynella Basket Press Cabernet/Merlot and Shiraz 1992 £6.49 each from Oddbins

Great evidence of Australia's new pride in 'old-fashioned' wine technology.

Chapel Hill Cabernet Sauvignon from Tesco, Thresher and AWC. The AWC will have Pam Dunsford's miraculous 1992 vintage which was voted best of the best at this year's Canberra show. At £8.99 it's deliciously suave and persuasive now but should get even better. The 1991 which Tesco are selling at £7.99 during December is also worth taking seriously and they are expected to stock the 1992 next spring. Poor old bordeaux 1991 and 1992 looks rather meagre alongside such concentrated gems.

Cape Mentelle Cabernet/Merlot 1992 £7.49 Majestic

This is the bargain from the Western Australian arm of the company that brought you Cloudy Bay, although alcohol freaks should be thrilled by the zany Zinfandel 1991 stocked by Adnams of Southwold at £8.95 and bargain hunters may prefer the cheaper Ironstone label.

Coldstream Hills Pinot Noir 1993 £8.49 Oddbins
Lavishly refinanced and on a medal-winning roll, this Victorian winery run by wine writer James Halliday has Australia's surest touch with the red burgundy grape - although Bannockburn can be damn fine too, as indeed is the Tasmanian Freycinet (join the waiting list on Boxford Wine 01787 210187).

Henschke Abbott's Prayer Merlot/Cabernet 1992 £12.95 Lay & Wheeler of Colchester
Very superior stuff apparently designed to win over those who find most Australian reds just too big for their boots.

Yeringberg Cabernets 1990 £13.75 Bibendum of London NW1
Gorgeously fashioned, serious, glossy, fine claret from a historic property in the Yarra Valley.

Yarra Yering Dry Reds £16.99 Oddbins
Majestically idiosyncratic, just like their maker the donnish Victorian Dr Bailey Carrodus

E & E Black Pepper Shiraz 1990/91 £13.49/12.75 Eckington Wines of Sheffield (01246 433213) and Oddbins Fine Wine.
This is the sort of strapping red, from two growers' old Barossa vines, the Aussies themselves fight over.

December 17, 1994

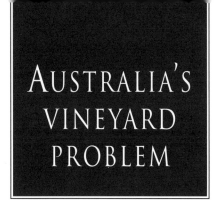

AUSTRALIA'S VINEYARD PROBLEM

'Cautious' and 'nervous' are two unlikely adjectives which accurately describe Australia's wine exporters at the moment. For the last few years they have been justifiably gung ho, with wine exports having risen tenfold since 1985 to represent almost one bottle in every four produced. Their much vaunted plan is to continue to woo overseas wine drinkers to the tune of A$1 billion by the year 2000, but they are hitting a few snags - even discounting a couple of natural disasters.

Frost dinted next year's vintage prospects in the all-important Barossa Valley, the most famous wine region in the wine state, South Australia. And a severe drought could well reduce the 1995 vintage in a country that is already short of the sort of premium grapes on which its export sales depend.

There has been a fury of new plantings, which will increase acreage by a good seven per cent (so much so that many fear there will be a grape glut in five years' time) but they will not come into production in time to halt a spiral in grape prices for the 1995 and 1996 vintages. Almost all wine producers depend heavily on grape growers, and paid them an average of 33 per cent more between June 1993 and June 1994, while average domestic wine prices rose just six per cent and export prices rose an almost unnoticeable one per cent.

Vines take three years to produce a viable crop, so plantings tend to reflect demand with a pronounced lag. Fuelled by 1980s fashions, everyone has been planting Chardonnay, so the most acute medium term shortages are predicted for premium red varieties such as Shiraz and Pinot Noir.

At the bottom end of the market, there is no lack of basic cheap Sultana and Muscat grapes (which alternate between supplying the wine and dried grape markets) and it could be that Australia's fate in the big bad wine world over the next year or so will depend on producers' resisting the temptation to stretch the good with the heavily irrigated distinctly less good.

(Australians, like many European wine producers, are allowed to blend in up to a total of 15 per cent of grapes, vintages and regions other than those specified on the label, but the catch-all South Eastern Australia appellation devised for export allows producers to source grapes more or less anywhere except the isolated and relatively limited vineyards of Western Australia.)

Australian wine folk, almost all of them male, are inveterate travellers. There is already considerable discontent within Australia that the 'flying winemaker' phenomenon, which sees antipodean winemakers making wine in Europe during their quiet winter back home, is simply diluting Australia's technical advantages by exporting them to its commercial rivals, many of them with lower cost bases.

Having themselves put pressure on the French in the late 1980s, Australian exporters are all too well aware of the increased competition their wines face from South America, South Africa, southern France and Eastern Europe in the mid 1990s. They have won a six per cent share of the precious UK market from a standing start, but on the basis of offering real value for money.

Many industry figures are concerned about how they will keep this enviable reputation as prices rise. "We have no alternative but to increase prices," maintains Robin Day, managing director of Pernod-Ricard's Orlando whose Jacobs' Creek range has become Britain's most popular brand of bottled wine. "We simply can't afford to absorb any more results of the currency movements and the grape shortage."

Brian Croser, who successfully negotiated a halt in the rise of domestic wine tax in late 1993, is also chairman of the commercially significant Royal Adelaide Wine Show. He had to report that this year's judging marathon resulted in a dramatic decrease in the number of gold medals awarded in the cheaper wine classes, of wines destined both for export and domestic markets.

"Australia has entered dangerous commercial territory," he warned his fellow wine producers. "The thing central to our success premium varietal wines at good prices - is vanishing. As the cost accountants rampage through our cellars, we are becoming producers of FAQ [fair average quality] wines. We must be careful as a viticultural nation that we don't lose sight of why our wines have been successful on export markets."

If by any chance the British did fall out of love with Australian wine (and nearly half of it exported from Australia/NZ went to the

UK last year), things could be very grim for the Australian wine market. The relatively static domestic market Down Under would find it extremely difficult to absorb the quantities involved without a repeat of the dumping which ruined the market in its last downswing.

December 24, 1994

Australia's 1995 harvest was down 10 to 25 per cent in terms of quantity, and vintners Down Under are hoping desperately for a bumper crop in 1996.

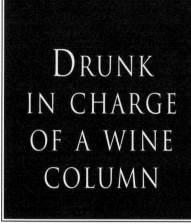

DRUNK
IN CHARGE
OF A WINE
COLUMN

I t was the 189th wine that really did me in. Not that there was anything inherently vicious about Mumm Cuvée Napa. Just that when you have, by an extreme exercise of will, managed to hold yourself together to taste nearly 200 wines by 3.30 in the afternoon, you tend to fall apart when you reach the last one.

I can just about decipher my tasting note "bit raw and sweet". But that is not to be taken as gospel, folks. I felt as though all I wanted to do was go home and enjoy a lovely long sleep, but by 6.30 I had to be in Westminster School's medieval dining hall, spouting forth knowledgeably about eight more wines.

Tuesday April 4 was an extremely silly day. There was not just one but two of the marathon wine tastings which British retailers now routinely organise in their attempts to maximise press coverage. The theory seems to be that the more bottles wine writers are exposed to, the greater the likelihood of their finding some, or at least one, they'll like sufficiently to mention in print.

So off I dutifully trotted to rinse my palate, first in Majestic's offerings at the University Women's Club in South Audley Street and then in Safeway's at the new Vintners' Place development in the City. But before any of that, indeed before breakfast, I have to "look at", as we say in and around the wine trade, three Chilean wines for an article to be despatched to these pages that very morning. So I have - I would not say I enjoy - my first wine of the day at 6.30 am.

But even worse, or better, or whatever it is, before I can get to those mass market wines, I have to go out to Hatton Cross near London airport and perform my duty as recently recruited wine consultant to British Airways.

By 9.30 Hugh Johnson, Master of Wine Colin Anderson and I (Michael Broadbent being in New York) have our heads down and noses in to 35 unidentified Spanish reds for Club Class. Once we agree on one (although not many more) gorgeous rioja, we then have to assess the relative maturity of five eye-wateringly young clarets so that BA's wine supremo Peter Nixson can plan in which order to allow these wines to fly away from his cache of bottles maturing for First Class and Concorde.

On the tube back to Green Park, fortified by BA sandwiches, I try to convince myself I am fighting fit and can hardly wait to get my teeth into the 108 wines Majestic have lined up in the university women's library (a most distracting location).

We wine scribes take time off between mouthfuls and note-taking to gossip, not about individual wines but about our colleagues' book advances.

I taste the 88 wines which most interest me (or rather, as I perceive it, you) and repair to the Ladies to try to rub some of the black stains off my teeth and fingers before trekking over to Safeway's line-up. On the pavement outside I meet a colleague who has decided to tackle the day's twin peaks in the reverse order. We sigh long-sufferingly about the absurdity of our workload and mark each others' cards. "Bulgaria's pretty good. They're all raving about the south of France, but I don't see it," is his verdict.

On to an empty suite of offices overlooking barges-full of London's detritus being shipped down the Thames where Safeway have opened an even more optimistic 120 bottles. A plate of bread and cheese helps but I can still manage only 58. The Cuvée Napa finally does me in.

When wine is tasted for work rather than pleasure, the aim is to experience all of the wine's characteristics except the fun bit, the alcohol. Accordingly, we look, we sniff, we swirl around our mouths and we then spit. But we inevitably absorb some alcohol as vapour, and even the most efficient spitter tends let some of the liquid dribble down the throat, however unintentionally.

I once experimented and found that the difference between what I'd take out into my mouth for 30 'tastes' and what I spat out was about a glassful, which suggests that by the time I reached wine number 189, I'd drunk the equivalent of nearly six glassfuls, or a bottle of wine. No wonder I was feeling so, what is the word, frail? Jaded? Involuntarily intoxicated? Drunk?

I reeled off to Bank tube station, happy to slump even in a Northern line carriage, for a few undisturbed, illiquid minutes. A bath slightly revived me, as did an early evening run from a taxi to Westminster because we got stuck in a traffic jam and were almost late for this wine tasting hooley I host annually for a solicitor friend.

The theme this year was 'Some of the Most Delicious Bottles in the World', and I can assure you that, despite the scores of wines already floating round my system, the Château Margaux 1983 (a silly £69.99 at Oddbins Fine Wine shops) hit it just as gracefully and inspirationally as it ever has done.

The solicitors were kind enough to say it was the best tasting ever. I don't remember dancing on the table, but I do remember one very direct result of all the wine I'd tasted. I, a maths graduate, somehow managed to tot the total number of wines I tasted up to 216 rather than than 197.

And the day after? Easy peasy. A mere two tastings and Hugh Johnson to dinner.

April 29, 1995